SPEAKING
BY THE
SPIRIT

...I WANT YOU TO KNOW THAT NO ONE WHO IS
SPEAKING BY THE SPIRIT SAYS, "JESUS BE
CURSED," AND NO ONE CAN SAY, "JESUS IS
LORD," EXCEPT BY THE HOLY SPIRIT.
1 COR 12:3 NIV

RON WOOD

Table of Contents

Bible References

Speaking by the Spirit

10 9 8 7 6 5 4 3 2 1

INTRODUCTION

CAN THE HOLY SPIRIT speak through a human being? My experience says, "Yes!" I've enjoyed and benefitted by the Holy Spirit helping me pray, worship, sing, intercede, and prophesy during these last sixty years. This began when I was about twelve. These are Spirit-filled expressions of speech either to God or to men.

Let's approach the question this way... what happens when two spirits inhabit the same body? This can occur. God is a spirit. His spirit can be inside our human body. His Spirit and my spirit are joined as one.

There are also bad spirits in this world. They can also get inside people. The Bible describes many such interactions. In the scriptures, there are numerous instances of people being moved upon, inhabited by, or receiving words from invisible spirits, both good and bad.

The spiritual realm is real. Heaven and hell both have agents here on the earth. There are wicked, evil spirits (*i.e.*- demons) who want to take disadvantage or harm human beings. These are unclean spirits. They plant vile imaginations, inflame perverted lusts, and insinuate evil propaganda into vulnerable people's minds.[1] They lie about God all the time.

Thankfully, there are also myriads of holy angels, messengers from God, who inhabit the spiritual dimension. They see the face of God. They help people. Although usually invisible, they can appear to us. We tend to be preoccupied with the material realm and don't notice spiritual beings. But you can be trained to discern.

You as a human being are spirit, soul, and body. As a person, you are a trinity. The following scripture bears this out. *Now may the God of peace Himself sanctify you entirely; and may your spirit and soul and body be preserved complete, without blame at the coming of our Lord Jesus Christ.* 1 Thess 5:23

In my practical theology, I describe our human trinity like this. With your *spirit* you relate to God. With your *soul* you relate to people. With your *body* you relate to the material world. Three Greek words in the New Testament text are used for these aspects: *pneuma, psuche,* and *soma.*

---

[1] For more on the biblical subject of Christ's victory over evil spirits see my book, *Deliverance - Our Legacy,* available on Amazon.com.

(spirit, soul, body) From the Greek we derive modern English words: pneumatic, psychology, and somatic.

I said all that to say this… You are an immortal spiritual being having a temporary human experience!

You live in two dimensions simultaneously. You can touch the spiritual realm, heaven, as well as live in this time-space material world, earth. When you worship God, you touch heaven. When God speaks, heaven touches you. One day, when Jesus returns to earth, we'll be translated into a glorious state. We'll get a resurrection body. We'll see him as he is, the king of Glory, God's Son, our Savior.

Jesus made a breath-taking promise to his followers as he prepared to ascend back to heaven. He said he would send to us "the promise of the Father." *And behold, I am sending forth the promise of My Father upon you; but you are to stay in the city until you are clothed with power from on high."* Luke 24:49

This event is already history. It happened when the Holy Spirit came upon 120 people on the day of Pentecost. (see Acts chapter 2) The Holy Spirit has come and he hasn't ever left. His presence is ongoing proof that Jesus returned to heaven and is now seated on his throne.

Therefore, having been exalted to the right hand of God, and having received from the Father the promise of the Holy Spirit, He has poured forth this which you both see and hear. Acts 2:33

That event, where God's presence impacted praying people, is when the church of Jesus Christ was born - the many-membered corporate body of Christ. That's us! No longer was God's manifest presence located in only one person, Jesus. The tangible presence of God, his glory, was dispersed to many, to all those who received Jesus. God, an eternal spirit, is now inhabiting all believers who place their trust in Jesus Christ. The Holy Spirit is now dwelling in many millions of mortal human beings.

So, you are in Christ and Christ is in you. Inside us, he bears witness to our identity, the fact of our adoption as heirs, our new family relationship. Even when you are not aware of it, by faith, you know that he is lives in your heart. He never leaves you. *"The anointing abides."* The Holy Spirit constantly indwells in your spirit. *"I will never leave you nor forsake you."* Like two breaths that are mingled together, you and he are one. *"He breathed on them and said, 'Receive Holy Spirit.'"* He guides you, comforts you, convicts you, convinces you, blesses you, enables you to pray, and empowers your worship. He even quickens the scriptures to you to help teach you about your heavenly Father's ways.

If God indwells you, what happens when he overflows through you? That's the topic of this book... how the divine over-flow works... when the Spirit of God infuses your spirit to speak.

I have noticed in the scriptures, especially in the Book of Acts, that every time a person or group was filled with the Spirit, the scripture records that something could be *seen or heard.* I invite you to study this for yourself. Don't take my word for it. There was always a manifestation that took place. *"...being full of the Spirit, he began to speak..."* It may be speaking in unknown tongues, or prophesying, or praising God, or it may be proclaiming the word of the Lord. It was observable, audible, and evidentiary. Onlookers were amazed.

The gift of the Holy Spirit is received purely by faith. But there are repeatable signs that can be expected to occur when ever this event happens. In the Bible, every time the Holy Spirit was imparted, received, or filled someone, onlookers saw something and heard something. Therefore, if there's nothing to see or nothing to hear, then likely nothing happened. You want the real deal, right? Don't stop seeking. Keep asking. Go back for another dip.

Jesus said the presence of the Holy Spirit would inhabit us and flow out from us like a river. *Now on the last day, the great day of the feast, Jesus stood and cried out, saying, "If anyone is thirsty, let him come to Me and drink. He who believes in Me, as the Scripture said, 'From his innermost being will flow rivers of living water.'" But this He spoke of the Spirit, whom those who believed in Him were to receive; for the Spirit was not yet given, because Jesus was not yet glorified.* John 7:37-39 NAS

This verse tells me that Jesus is the Baptizer. He is the source, the fountainhead of the Spirit. If you are thirsty for more of God, the solution is simple. Come to Jesus. He satisfies the thirsty. He won't send hungry people away fasting or empty. Get desperate for more of God.

Something inside us is meant to flow out from us. It is meant to flow like a river. That something is the Spirit of God. Believers are designed to drink continuously from the river of life in Jesus. I can imagine, like anything else, that if we happen to get full enough, we will surely overflow. A flowing river spreads life everywhere it goes.

As regenerated Christians, we bear the likeness of our Creator. We have the DNA of our Father in heaven. We are image-bearers of God because of Christ who dwells in us, the hope of glory. Wherever we go, the Lord goes with us. To a degree, we resemble our older brother, Jesus.

One trait of God is that he speaks. He is not silent. He wants us to listen to him and he wants us to speak for him. We are not silent creatures. We can communicate. We can choose to speak words. No other animal has this marvelous gift - the capacity to speak clearly. Based on many scriptures, it is obvious that the Holy Spirit, who is God, is a speaking spirit. *"Hear what the Spirit is saying to the churches."* (Rev. 2:17) The "is" in the text is present tense. He is here and He is not mute.

Therefore I make known to you that no one speaking by the Spirit of God says, "Jesus is accursed"; and no one can say, "Jesus is Lord," except by the Holy Spirit. 1 Cor. 12:3

You and I can say things. Humans can talk. What words will we say? There are three sources of speech. God, our mind, or spirits. A person can speak. Nonpersons cannot. We can be infused with God and speak his words. Based on this scripture and numerous examples in the Bible, we know that people can speak by the Spirit. Later I'll explain the mechanism of precisely how this happens; whether it's the Spirit speaking directly through human agency or a person speaking while being prompted with words coming from the Holy Spirit.

When the Spirit speaks, we call it prophetic utterance.[2]

In this book, I use certain terms that you should know. These are *prophecy, prophesy, prophetic utterance*, and *prophet.*

1) A *prophecy* is a noun, a thing. "She gave a prophecy" (pro-fess-E). It is a word that was spoken.

2) To *prophesy* is a verb, an action. "I felt led to prophesy" (pro-fess-I). This is something we speak by the Spirit.

3) A *prophetic utterance* is a word, a message spoken aloud by a believer that is delivered under the inspiration or the prompting of the Spirit. "He gave us a prophetic word." In this book you will learn how to be used of God to deliver a prophetic word to the church or to an individual.

---

[2] For those wanting more theology about charismatic gifts or the baptism in the Holy Spirit, I recommend some good evangelical Bible scholars such as Gordon Fee (*God's Empowering Presence*), Wayne Grudem, (*Systematic Theology*), Jack Deere (*Surprised by the Voice of God*), and Derek Prince (*The Spirit-Filled Believer's Handbook*). There are many others.

4) A *prophet* is a person, a five-fold minister who is gift of Christ to the church. They stand in the office or the calling of a prophet. I'll show you how to identity them.

You'll learn later that not everyone who prophesies is a prophet (most are not), and you'll learn how to evaluate prophetic words that you hear or receive. You should also know that many prophets don't pastor churches. Nor do they necessarily live off of their ministry even though they are entitled to be supported by tithes and offerings like any other workers Jesus sends. Many are tentmakers like Paul. Prophets in their day job may be teachers, or ranchers, or retired folks.

The biblical gift of prophecy is a supernatural activity of the Holy Spirit. It is intended for the life of every Christian, not just for preachers. It is meant to operate in the body of Christ for our mutual edification. Its absence is a profound drag on the church.

However, if you want to activate this wonderful gift in your life as Paul clearly instructs us to do, there must be a whole new level of teaching, training and equipping within the church. The doctrine of the word is meant to accompany the activity of the Spirit. Like any powerful spiritual gift, prophecy can be a blessing. If misused, it can cause confusion. So let's go back to school and let the Lord teach us!

Problems in the church with the gift of prophecy can occur due to character defects in the gifted person. The vessel can contaminate the gift. This may have roots in their personality or upbringing. They can cause problems if they need to dominate, or lack humility, are insecure, are repeatedly rude, or missed practical training in the use of spiritual gifts. Character is a big issue with the Lord. We all need to know proper biblical protocol. People who don't walk in love shouldn't be prophesying.

Pursue love, yet desire earnestly spiritual gifts, but especially that you may prophesy. (1 Cor 14:1) Notice three important things in this brief passage.

<u>One:</u> Don't leave love out. God doesn't need angry prophets. His words flow out of love. Love is God's nature.

<u>Two:</u> Desire spiritual gifts. This means actively go after them. Don't sit back passively waiting for them to arrive. They won't drop in your lap. Chase after them.

<u>Three:</u> Especially covet (desire or seek after) the ability to prophecy. Prophecy is special. There is a reason for this – it edifies the church the most, more so than any other spiritual gift. By the way, the word "desire" is a very strong word. We are told to covet this gift. I like to translate this in modern vernacular: *"Crave the things of the Spirit."*

CHURCHES AND PROPHECY

IN MY OPINION, training to deploy prophetic gifts in the church should be in place *before* inaugurating this ministry. If not, some flaky prophet wannabees or immature amateur exhorters will surely sow havoc among the saints. The resulting chaos is not worth it. However, this is totally avoidable. That's why I'm writing this book, to help people avoid unnecessary trouble.

That's why this book is another in my series of training materials. I want to leave a legacy. I recommend that serious students of the Bible who desire to prophesy obtain some of these books and read them thoughtfully before going any further. Be a student of the scriptures. Learn from the mistakes of others. I've made so many errors, I'm an expert! Be attuned to the Lord's voice for yourself before you try to hear God for anyone else.

Are you ready? Let's assume as you study this material that several things have already happened in your life. Besides having a walk with the Lord that includes daily Bible reading and prayer, let me list some basics. However, realize that the things of the Spirit such as hearing God's voice, prophesying, and praying in the Spirit begin before you're fully mature. Babies get gifts!

• You are born of the Spirit. This means being alive toward God.

• Your life has been discipled by God so that you live submitted to God's will and you try to honor Jesus as your Lord. Being discipled includes following the Lord in water baptism. Baptism is an authority thing. It's the entryway into the church.

• You are bearing fruit by walking in the Spirit to the degree that those who know you can see Christlikeness in your character. You also have chosen to forgive those who have offended you.

• You have received your personal Pentecost (*i.e.*- baptism in the Holy Spirit) and are filled to overflowing, praising the Lord.

• You are involved in a local church so that mature believers and godly shepherds over the flock know you and love you.

If these things are *not* your present reality, then please read no further. You are not yet ready to be trusted with the gifts of the Spirit, especially prophetic utterance. Go back to school. Do the basics so that you qualify. Earn the respect of your pastors and leaders in the church. Grow in your hunger for the things of God. Practice praying in private before you dare try to speak in public.

As a Christian pastor, missionary, and Bible teacher with over fifty years of church experience among Spirit-filled people, I suppose I could add another topic as a prerequisite for those eager to prophesy: *be accountable or else be quiet.* This is a requirement. No exemptions!

You know I'm joking but I'm also serious. I know several wonderful Spirit-filled pastors with healthy churches who wouldn't dream of making room for the Spirit's gifts, especially prophecy, in any of their worship services. Why? Because some of their members are unruly, untaught, or undisciplined. Their pastors, wisely, are afraid to turn them loose. It could open a can of worms. It could split the church. If I were them, I would be cautious too, unless certain conditions are met first. Those conditions involve training selected disciples to operate this gift.

Actually, this sad condition – the absence of prophecy – is a reality in most congregations today. This weighs heavily on my heart. Rarely today will you ever hear a prophetic word from the Lord in a church service, not even in Pentecostal or charismatic churches, much less in mainline evangelical churches. This is a deficiency. There is a reason for this. And it is not God's fault.

Maybe the denomination's colleges or seminaries are not teaching students the whole Bible. Their traditions have ruled this out. But usually the absence of any prophesying by Christians in a particular church is the local leader's fault. The man in charge, the senior pastor, very likely, has been repressing this spiritual gift. Or he has failed to equip the saints with the biblical knowledge they need to minister this delightful gift.

This may be due to the pastor not having experienced it for himself. Perhaps the leader won't attempt to train his church because prophecy is not his strong suit. That's understandable. You can't lead people where you haven't been. Maybe he (or she) doesn't have an ally, a prophetic teacher whom they can trust to help introduce this gift's operation to their church. Maybe they haven't seen it demonstrated in a wholesome way. Maybe the church board has a tight grip on the reins and is saying, "Don't rock the boat." There may be other reasons why prophecy in a particular church is forbidden or neglected. The bottom line is, the people are missing out on what this dynamic edifying ministry of the Spirit can supply.

I can honestly say, based on widely varied church situations over fifty years of ministry, I've seen many believers deliver awesome supernatural edifying prophecies. Real prophesy always takes things to a higher level in God. The reverse is also true. As the actor in the State Farm TV commercial says, "We know a thing or two because we've seen a thing or two." I've seen it all too: the good, the bad, and the ugly. When it's good, there's nothing better. I've also witnessed some crazy hilarious flops that were a huge failure. I've been on the receiving end of some weird ones. However, with proper biblical instruction, you can turn misfires into practical lessons on prophetic protocol. There is no need to throw the baby out with the bathwater.

My advice to my pastor friends is this: If you want the good kind of powerfully edifying prophetic ministry in your church, there is a right way to do it. Healthy prophecy occurs in safe pastoral settings. Ask a seasoned, proven prophet or reputable Bible teacher experienced in these things to come work alongside you in your congregation, your conference, or your home group. Small group sessions, classes and workshops are an ideal format. Have a controlled learning environment where people are free to ask questions, experiment, and make mistakes. Discover who among your members is gifted.

Find a helper, specialist, or gifted person who will bless your church; someone who will work as a teammate under your direction to accomplish this task. You want someone who will honor the pastor's comfort level. Use good training materials. Be patient. It takes time. You don't want a false start. Lay a solid foundation. Train only a few to begin with. Deploy a pilot group under close supervision at first. Start small and develop a working model, then expand from there. Use pastoral wisdom.

Pastors know to walk carefully, move deliberately. Don't spook the sheep. Lead the sheep to green pastures and to still waters. Shepherds carefully feed the sheep. They don't drive them like cattle or push them. Sheep move best at a slow steady pace.

In actuality, pastors are the gatekeepers who can permit or prohibit the gifts of the Spirit. But pastors need help. Have a specialist come alongside. That's why there are five ministries of Christ listed in Ephesians 4:11, not just one.

And He gave some as apostles, and some as prophets, and some as evangelists, and some as pastors and teachers, for the equipping of the saints for the work of service, to the building up of the body of Christ... Eph 4:11-12

Have you ever considered this? Pastors are just one among the five ministries of Christ. The gospel ministry is not meant to be a one man show. Solo ministry is asking too much of any single person. It is unbiblical and unworkable. Burnout is the main reason why so many pastors leave the ministry after only a few years.

Why five varieties of ministry? They are all needed to equip the saints so they can do their ministry. It takes all five or else they'll be deficient. These five headship ministries have a goal above all others - equip the saints. If they fail, then they are failures.

...for the equipping of the saints for the work of service, to the building up of the body of Christ.... (Eph 4:12) This is how the Lord of the church measures success in the ministry for his workers. They equip the members.

Each of the five ascension gift offices carries and imparts a distinct grace that equips the saints. Each does it in a different way than the other four. To have the fulness of Christ expressed, we need all five of these ministry gifts active in the church. They are not interchangeable. Each is a specialist. No single solo minister is meant to be a superman. No leader can quip or mature the saints alone. All five (apostles, prophets, evangelists, pastors, and teachers) have a part to play that is essential. They are like the colors in a rainbow that make up the spectrum of light.

Have you noticed when Jesus sent out workers, he sent them in pairs? That the apostles all had teams? Don't go it alone. We truly need one another. Pastors and prophets are not interchangeable. We're not all alike. Ministers are meant to team up. There is power there.

The precautions and suggestions I've listed above are meant to add some practical wisdom for those believers who are worshipping in congregational settings, by that I mean the institutional church. This is the most common church structure extant in modern America. It is perhaps the most difficult organizational structure of all in which to encourage the gift of prophecy. Why? Because it can interfere with preaching.

A congregation usually has one lead pastor. It is often in a denominational hierarchy or in a network of churches, perhaps with a bishop, overseer, or superintendent. Some churches are stand alone, being independent, and don't connect well with others. Congregations are typically a hundred people to a few thousand. They usually meet in church facilities or bigger arenas.

I graduated from an evangelical Bible college, Southeastern University, in Lakeland, Florida. It was an excellent Spirit-filled school. I loved the knowledge I gained about the Bible and church history. I found a jewel there - my bride! I majored in Missiology but had enough credit hours to major in Bible. I went from there directly into the full-time ministry, pastoring a small church. I soon discovered that I had not been equipped to start a church, only to step into a church that was already begun. I had been trained to run a Christian business called a congregation.

Now you'll see in the section ahead that I seem to take a side trail to talk about congregations and house churches. This isn't a detour. It's a necessary word picture so you won't face disappointment as you begin praying and asking the Lord to allow you to experience the spiritual gift of prophecy. You'll discover that prophesying by the Spirit is not very welcome in most organized churches. In fact, the two things that the apostle Paul urged all Christians to do the most (pray and prophesy) (1 Tim 2:1) and 1 Cor 14:1) are not easily done in any of our institutional church situations. I know this is true because that is the kind of church I led for most of my ministry career.

How do churches begin? The Lord showed me how but that's a story for another book. God uses small things to grow big things. He uses two or three who agree. If a church is small, say about 10-20 people, it can be an assembly that meets in a house, like a cell church. You can spot these house churches all through the New Testament.

But Saul began ravaging the church, entering house after house... (Acts 8:30) *...also greet the church that is in their house.* (Rom 16:5) *Aquila and Prisca greet you heartily in the Lord, with the church that is in their house.* (1 Cor 16:19) What was the common denominator of these churches? They met in homes.

When I planted a new church, that was the model I used. I began with a band of believers meeting in a home. Most church growth scholars use the term "organic church" as opposed to meeting in a special facility, a church building. Whatever the system they utilized, in the New Testament pattern, the organic church always included four ingredients: *teaching, prayer, fellowship, and breaking bread.* This is described in Acts 2.

*Peter said to them, "Repent, and each of you be baptized in the name of Jesus Christ for the forgiveness of your sins; and you will receive the gift of the Holy Spirit. For the promise is for you and your children and for all who are far off, as many as the Lord our God will call to Himself." And with many other words he solemnly testified and kept on exhorting them, saying, "Be saved from this perverse generation!" So then, those who had received his word were baptized; and that day there were added about three thousand souls. They were continually devoting themselves to the **apostles' teaching** and to **fellowship**, to the **breaking of bread** and to **prayer**.* Acts 2:38-41

Peter had preached, *"Be saved from this perverse generation!"* Three thousand people responded. What does it mean to live in the midst of a crooked, twisted, perverse generation? How is anyone saved from a culture that's demonized, that butchers its unborn young, that has lost its morality and is disconnected from truth? The answer is the gospel, the good news, that Christ is risen and alive, and that his kingdom has arrived. But the gospel's practical outworking was a new kingdom counterculture. This is the way to do it. This is the new apostolic imperative that saves us from the lostness of the surrounding world. It begins with the gospel but ends with the church. What rescues us? Living the daily life of the local church with its orthodox habits preserves us.

There was no building to put the new people into. How did the Twelve care for them? *So then, those who had received his word were baptized; and that day there were added about three thousand souls.* They had a big problem: the huge number of converts! What to do?

The new converts had to be discipled by the apostles. They immediately began training them using the pattern of Jesus. Jesus started small, with twelve men. These disciples, Jesus' primary agents, now began teaching and training the newly baptized 3,000 converts. *They were continually devoting themselves to the apostles' teaching and to fellowship, to the breaking of bread and to prayer.* (2:42) These four elements (**teaching, fellowship, breaking bread, and prayer**) comprised the basic life of the local church. This is how the new disciples lived. They were the church. They did not go to church. There was no church building to go to!

From the evidence here and in many other passages, I believe the new church in Acts 2 began meeting in the homes of the believers. The persecution by the Jews eventually drove them away from the Temple. Later Christians were expelled from the synagogues. The new church of Jesus Christ had left the building. The temporary temple gatherings or any congregation-style meetings served a transition purpose while the apostles trained the disciples how to be the church (rather than go to church). In fact, in the original New Testament Greek language, there's no way to say, "Let's go to church."

After a while the closest thing to large church gatherings was when Paul travelled to a city and gathered the elders together in a public place. Why? Because the crowd was too big for a typical home. But he also met with them in their homes. This pattern was clear in Ephesus.

*...how I did not shrink from declaring to you anything that was profitable, and teaching you **publicly** and from **house to house**, solemnly testifying to both Jews and Greeks of repentance toward God and faith in our Lord Jesus Christ.* Acts 20:20

The early church didn't have congregations anchored to physical buildings. They had organic churches that met in homes. Every member of the church shared their experience of Christ when they gathered weekly, with no single preacher or professional clergy dominating the meeting. The disciples networked together. They met in homes. The roving apostles stopped by occasionally. It was one diverse church with many modules in each city.

For our modern denominational churches that have stopped growing and yet wonder why, this is the elephant in the room. That, and rejecting the baptism in the Holy Spirit. Wrong structure *and* a missing dynamic. For the Pentecostals and charismatics who have stopped growing, it's because they're stuck in old wineskins that keep all the ministry in the hands of the paid clergy. This silences the members. I know about this personally because for decades I was part of the problem.[3]

Now, you may wonder why I said so much about church structures when my goal is to teach about prophesying. The reason is the beautiful gifts of praying in the Spirit and prophesying doesn't work well in artificial settings. Religious programs and rigid agendas kill it. The members of Christ's body are muzzled, leaving only the paid professionals to minister. The living vine of Christ's body withers and dies when it's kept in a box.

On the other hand, members of the church can pray and speak when their structure allows it. They can even sing by the Spirit! *And do not get drunk with wine, for that is dissipation, but be filled with the Spirit, speaking to one another in psalms and hymns and spiritual songs, singing and making melody with your heart to the Lord;* (Eph 5:18-19) But today the prophetic song of the Spirit is mostly silent, replaced by a choir and talented musicians.

---

[3] The topic of church structures deserves more careful attention.

HOUSE CHURCHES

EPHESUS HAD MANY hundreds of house churches, perhaps with 30,000 total members. The word of God was prevailing in Ephesus. Idolatry and unbelief were being defeated in that city as the gospel multiplied house churches. House churches are normal and good. They are usually healthy unless they become isolated or ingrown. A house church is a legitimate expression of the body of Christ. House churches are biblical and orthodox.

I want to see all believers brought into a healthier expression of the life of Christ, both personally and in community. *Koinonia* (community, fellowship) means life shared together in Jesus. That's the reason why I explain how house churches work. Congregations meeting in buildings are a modern development. I'm not against congregations – they are important, especially as they become apostolic centers to train and equip believers and send out more workers, and as they become "charging stations" for believers to be filled with the Spirit. But they need to redefine their mission and adapt. The church in Acts had only a few large gatherings, such as outside the Temple in the courtyard and later in the school of Tyrannus. But these were infrequent apostolic teaching sessions which differed from the routine life of the church.

In this book my focus is not to teach about church structures or apostolic ministry; that's incidental. But it's helpful to know that there are alternatives to the routine non-biblical church in a box. A variety of methods is not heresy. Orthodoxy is right beliefs, but we need to discover orthopraxy, right practices. Be flexible but be practical. God is practical. As Dr. Phil says, "How's that been working for you?"

Where's the fruit? Can we measure the results? Whatever you call them – home Bible studies, prayer meetings, cells, life groups, life circles, neighborhood prayer watches, or simple churches – they work well with supervision. They are perhaps a step in the right direction. They can provide a taste of more freedom. They can be part of the *oikos* of the church. They can provide order plus liberty for spiritual gifts. The mature church, with some apostolic direction, can meet successfully without any paid staff being required. That's the highest goal... every member ministering.

The relational dynamics of a house church are very different from a large congregation that meets in a religious building or a big auditorium. The *group dynamics* of big meetings are better suited to teaching and training, not for exercising gifts. This larger group method was used by Paul when circumstances led him to teach (actually, train for trainers) for a span of two years at a local school owned by Tyrannus in Ephesus.

And he entered the synagogue and continued speaking out boldly for three months, reasoning and persuading them about the kingdom of God. But when some were becoming hardened and disobedient, speaking evil of the Way before the people, he withdrew from them and took away the disciples, reasoning daily in the school of Tyrannus. This took place for two years, so that all who lived in Asia heard the word of the Lord, both Jews and Greeks. Acts 19:8-10

The apostle's foundational ministry (kingdom dynamics training) was temporary, intense, and targeted. It was more than intellectual doctrine but included the power of the Holy Spirit. This lasted two years. Then the elders took over in their house churches. I've studied this cycle that I call "The Revival at Ephesus" for forty years. It was a major turnaround event. It was likely one of the best combinations of the word and the Spirit ever presented. In another of my books, I try to explain why Paul was ready for what had to be done in Ephesus, using my illustration of his ministry career progression.

Under the apostle Paul, the church had left the synagogue. It was a practical decision. He left the religious structure and rented a school. From there, all of that region heard the word of God. Something was causing the gospel to multiply. His strategy was working in a way we don't often see now. Yet Paul remained at the hub, his apostolic center. It was his disciples that were spreading the word. What can this method teach us?

It is my conviction that church buildings ought to be devoted to mission, not maintenance. The church needs prophetic impetus to become more apostolic. We need the dynamic of the Spirit so we can break out of our cocoon.

For Paul at Ephesus training workers in the rented school building, it was like he was telling his disciples, *"You have two years to get out of here!"* His apostolic mandate was not to fill up a building. It was not to gather a bigger and bigger crowd. No! He was training and equipping new workers to send them out. Ultimate success is in having successors. Paul was determined to work himself out of a job. His legacy would last beyond his lifetime. The work was too big for him to do alone. If we get in a hurry or think short term, we'll do the expedient instead of the important. Paul trained disciples.

The church needs to rediscover its apostolic thrust. The daily life of the church should expand out of the building, beyond four walls, into every arena of human life and endeavor. The kingdom needs to drive the devil out of society. The gospel needs to take over. House groups can easily proliferate throughout a whole city. Everywhere that members of the church live or work can be a lighthouse for God. More and more workers can receive training on the job, which is our gospel task, "each one reach one," winning more souls, planting more organic churches. Jesus' kingdom has no limits.

If you already own a building or have a large church auditorium, don't burn it down. Don't sell it. Just repurpose it. Repristinate it. Rediscover the kingdom. Get out of your box canyon. Key leaders can train workers and equip disciples. Apostles can multiply their ministry. The maturing believers can multiply affordable, friendly home groups where evangelism and pastoral care naturally occurs. This is an apostolic strategy. It can spread quickly and cheaply. It puts the members of the whole church to work. It is so rewarding and so much fun.

Buildings never were the church. The people, individuals who belong to Jesus, they are the church! Where the church is meeting is incidental. The body of Christ is organic. It's a living body with many connected members possessing many different gifts.

House churches are becoming very common around the world. They work in China and Pakistan. They work in Colombia and Cuba. Church planters can bypass the cost and challenges of buying property or acquiring a building. Persecution against public meetings and the increasing expense of facilities dictate this. Besides that, house churches train new gospel leaders rapidly. Have apprentices. Give quality instruction to a small band. If you do it right, it won't stay small for long. House churches divide in order to multiply. They were the historic model for the early church during the first three centuries of Christianity. House gatherings are typically the kind of meeting mentioned in the New Testament whenever Paul met with the church in a city.

The shepherds of house churches will gather with an apostle to be trained, as happened with the elders of Ephesus who met with Paul. (Acts 20:17) The church in the city met in many places using different homes. The elders all knew one another. (20:28) They all worked together as a team. In these home settings, the Spirit of the Lord was in charge. Many believers could minister their gifts as the Spirit led. There was no single preacher dominating the meeting with a sermon. This is more flexible and impromptu than any large congregation can ever be. It is the New Testament pattern, a divine matrix in which Jesus is head of his body the church, and every member may be blessed to pray, prophesy, and share.

Why are prophesying and praying (activities of the Spirit) more acceptable in smaller house churches? These meetings are informal. They have spontaneity. No one is in charge but the Lord Jesus. They aren't organized around a tight schedule or built around a seminarian's sermon or rigidly celebrating the ritual liturgy of the eucharist. They do share a common meal at which they also enjoy the Lord's Supper. The discuss the apostles' teaching found in the scriptures. They pray together for God's kingdom to come. They minister to one another in prayer and by using the gifts of the Holy Spirit. They help each other and they give offerings to the poor.

This kind of church is like a family. Therefore, when the Spirit moves in an informal home setting with a prophetic utterance or a word of revelation, it is easier to go with the flow and receive it, then evaluate it afterwards in the discussion time that follows. It is simple, organic, relational. People love each another. The listen to each other. Every member can minister. They aren't religious but real. This is *kingdom koinonia*, the church.

Here's how Paul described a typical house church meeting.... *What is the outcome then, brethren? When you assemble, each one has a psalm, has a teaching, has a revelation, has a tongue, has an interpretation. Let all things be done for edification. If anyone speaks in a tongue, it should be by two or at the most three, and each in turn, and one must interpret; but if there is no interpreter, he must keep silent in the church; and let him speak to himself and to God. Let two or three prophets speak, and let the others pass judgment. But if a revelation is made to another who is seated, the first one must keep silent. For you can all prophesy one by one, so that all may learn and all may be exhorted; and the spirits of prophets are subject to prophets; for God is not a God of confusion but of peace, as in all the churches of the saints.* 1 Cor 14:16-33

Prophesy was one of the main features of their regular meetings. This last phrase, "in all the churches of the saints," shows that this pattern of corporate ministry with free expression of the *pneumatikos* (spiritual gifts) was a common form of New Testament Christian community.

You can see in this passage, as each member contributed, that there was a protocol for the exercise of prophetic gifts in the home meeting. It was not without accountability or oversight, as each house church had elders (older members) or shepherds over the flock. Ideally, the shepherds were all joined to a travelling apostle. I've been in this kind of meeting and I've hosted them. They are delightful. In Paul's pattern, all of the people took turns sharing what the Holy Spirit was giving them. The ministry was done by the people, not by the pastor. There was no paid clergyman with a busy schedule who was preaching to an audience of listeners on pews. Instead, the body of Christ was ministering to itself.

This was the expected outcome when believers met in informal house meetings, having all been filled with the Holy Spirit. Everyone there could prophesy. It was mutual, cooperative, full of love, and edifying. The people were being naturally supernatural. This kind of Christ-community was wildly attractive for new people who wanted to be part of it. God was there! Their faith grew. They grew numerically. It spontaneously increased without any programs, buses, budgets, or buildings.

This is what was meant by this verse in Ephesians…. *from whom the whole body, being fitted and held together by what every joint supplies, according to the proper working of each individual part, causes the growth of the body for the building up of itself in love.* (Eph 4:16 NAS). This is "body ministry." They fit and they functioned.

Sounds scary doesn't it? Let's admit it, our religious methods and traditions are quenching the Spirit. We've stifled the saints; hobbled the work horses. To be specific, our wineskin won't stretch. It is not flexible. It limits our ministry. It is not just our doctrine, but traditional structures that inhibit our growth.

What to do? I say, hold on to the historic truth of the Bible, keep our good doctrines, and continue to confess our ancient church creeds. But adopt a flexible wineskin, a new way of a being the church; one where the saints may freely minister by the Spirit. Break out of your box!

The Holy Spirit likes to break out of any box that we try to keep him in. The vine runs over the walls. The Holy Spirit wants to liberate believers so they can hear from him and thus speak by the Spirit. This is what the Bible means by the gift of prophecy. The residual voice of the Spirit is always singing in our hearts. Once you know this, the rest is a learned skill. You grow by trying it, getting trained, and walking in the wisdom of humility.

WHEN BELIEVERS PROPHESY

WHAT IS PROPHESYING? Start with the basics. It is a spiritual gift, not a natural talent nor is it human training. Here is what the apostle Paul said when he wrote to the Corinthians about this important manifestation of the Holy Spirit.

Now there are varieties of gifts, but the same Spirit. And there are varieties of ministries, and the same Lord. There are varieties of effects, but the same God who works all things in all persons. But to each one is given the manifestation of the Spirit for the common good. For to one is given the word of wisdom through the Spirit, and to another the word of knowledge according to the same Spirit; to another faith by the same Spirit, and to another gifts of healing by the one Spirit, and to another the effecting of miracles, and to another prophecy, and to another the distinguishing of spirits, to another various kinds of tongues, and to another the interpretation of tongues. But one and the same Spirit works all these things, distributing to each one individually just as He wills. 1 Cor 12:4-11 NAS

Let me highlight a few points that Paul enumerated here. These manifestations are called *gifts*. Notice, three of the nine gifts are verbal- tongues, interpretation, and prophecy. Praying and preaching are verbal expressions which are greatly augmented by being filled with the Spirit. Gifts are a big doctrine but often ignored. They always come by grace and are always received by faith. They also operate by faith. More on that later.

Because *charismata* (manifestations of the Holy Spirit) arrive as a gift, not a merit badge, they don't come by achievement, excellence, or maturity. It is not an award or something you earn. It is a blessing that you receive. That means young people, children, or untaught believers can receive them. Therefore, we need to be evaluating prophetic words since inexperienced believers will express them partly right and partly wrong.

Notice how often the word *variety* appears. There is no one way to do this, except they all must operate in love. The Lord creates unique people, unique ministries, and unique churches. When the Lord has his way, we will need to throw away the cookie cutters and the spread sheets.

Notice how Paul emphasizes that it is the *same* Spirit. The gifts are not different spirits acting on different people, but the same Holy Spirit. All these amazing variations of charismatic gifts expressed through believers come from one Holy Spirit. He distributes them to individuals for everyone's benefit. The gifts are for the *common good*. If I have a gift in my life, it is not for me, it is meant to help others. That's why you might see a person with a grace-gift for healing become ill, yet when they pray for other people, they get healed even while he or she is still sick. I've seen this happen.

Notice that the gifts are called *manifestations*. They are overflowing eruptions of what a believer is carrying internally. When the gifts are dormant, they are invisible. When they are stirred up, they can be noticed. They are audible or visible. If these gifts aren't being manifested, then no one is being blessed. That is why we should stir up these dormant gifts. An inactive gift goes to waste. While inactive, it doesn't go away; it just sits on a shelf. Gifts are never recalled by God.

Among these many gifts is the best gift of all – prophecy, which is superior to the others because of its great power to edify the church.

Prophecy is not just preaching nor is it just teaching, although it may have elements of these at times. *But now, brethren, if I come to you speaking in tongues, what will I profit you unless I speak to you either by way of revelation or of knowledge or of prophecy or of teaching?* 1 Cor 14:6

Peter said that those who preach the gospel may do so by the Holy Spirit. They were speaking by the Spirit. *It was revealed to them that they were not serving themselves, but you, in these things which now have been announced to you through those who preached the gospel to you by the Holy Spirit sent from heaven—things into which angels long to look.* (1 Pet 1:12) When you hear someone speaking God's word by the Spirit – under the anointing – you will know it! I love Spirit-inspired preaching. We need more of it along with more biblical teaching that is practical and useful.

In contrast to tongues, prophecy (like preaching or teaching) imparts things immediately knowable to the hearer. What is said in tongues remains a mystery, unless it is interpreted. As Paul said, *"For if I pray in an unknown tongue, my spirit prayeth, but my understanding is unfruitful."* (1 Cor 14:14 KJV) In order to learn, people need to understand the words that are being spoken.

HOW I BEGAN PROPHESYING

SINCE WE ARE discussing speaking in tongues in the context of prophesying, let me make a point about why *glossalia* is such a rich source of blessing. I discovered early on in my walk with the Lord, after I was baptized in the Holy Spirit, that praying in tongues was often a prelude to prophesying. I could edify myself or build myself up during my time of worshipping in the Spirit. This was in my private devotions. In those days, I think it was an advantage for me to be raised among Pentecostals. Gifts of the Holy Spirit were very common among them.

I often sought God in prayer by entreating or praising him both alone and in corporate prayer meetings. I would walk and pray or kneel and pray and easily lose track of time. During those days I was surprised to discover that the initial experience I had when I first received the gift of the Spirit, worshipping in unknown tongues, was repeatable. I could yield to God again whenever I wanted to and flow again in unknown tongues. This added to my prayer experience and helped me greatly. I practiced this kind of private prayer very often. My inner man or my spirit man was edified even though my mind could not understand what my heart was saying. It felt so liberating! I found that giving expression to this gift in adoration to God was very refreshing and delightful.

Later, in the church meetings, the Lord began to use me to occasionally speak forth what was called back then, "a message in unknown tongues." This was declared aloud to the congregation at the appropriate time, when there was a pause as we waited on the Lord. It was quite dramatic. Someone else would interpret the word I gave. Over time, I began to interpret someone else's word or even interpret the word I had just spoken. Later still, among charismatic home prayer meetings and in Spirit-filled churches, I began to speak forth in prophecy to the group, even though no tongues had been spoken aloud prior. The message in tongues and interpretation seemed equivalent to prophecy. I am convinced that praying in heavenly tongues privately helped me publicly express prophetic words in English. The verbal gifts of the Spirit seem to be connected. It all had the same source.

Years later I began my preaching ministry. After days-long sessions of intense Bible study and preparation, I would spend at least an hour praying in the Spirit before I went out to preach to the congregation. I noticed that there were times when my private praying in tongues seemed to have a cadence or rhythm to it. Later as I spoke to the church, that same style was incorporated into my preaching. It stood out to me even though I'm sure no one else noticed it. It was like the Lord was helping this inexperienced minister be able to preach better by letting him rehearse in the Spirit what he would soon be saying in English to the church.

Here's one other point that may intrigue people who are prophetic or who hunger to prophesy. All of my initial prophetic ministry was to crowds - to churches meeting as large congregations. The experience of prophesying to a big congregation had its own peculiar dynamics. I would sense an unction come on me. My heart rate would go up. I would get hot or sweat. There was a physical feeling as the anointing came on me. I suppose this is what the ancient prophets meant when they said, "The hand of the Lord was upon me." It was a strong sensation. The word of the Lord would grow bigger inside me, like a fountain welling up, like a bubble wanting to burst. It felt like a fire in my bones. Later I said humorously, "If you get a word like that, you have to let it out or it'll hurt you!" I needed that special unction in order to project a powerful word to a large crowd. When it was done, I was done, and I would sit down, exhausted.

Later, the Lord began to guide me to prophesy to individuals. These expressions had more words of knowledge, words of wisdom, or personal encouragement than did the congregational words. To be honest, I had a lot of difficulty stepping into this new mode. It is not hard now. Now it flows easily. But back then in the beginning, I felt put on the spot. Before, I was never bothered by the opportunity to prophesy to a crowd of a thousand, but one little grandmother in tennis shoes standing in front of me intimidated me. Over time, after a lot of struggle, I found out why. I was waiting for the special unction, the hand of God to be on me, the fire in my bones. But that wasn't needed for serving personal prophecies to individuals.

If I had prophesied like that, with the "thus saith the Lord" style necessary for huge crowds, it would have hit the individual like a fire hose. They would have been plastered up against a wall. Instead, I learned to dial it down, lower my volume, speak softly, go slow, be gentle, as though I were kneeling at their feet serving them a word on a tray with a towel over my arm. In this gentler mode, I could follow the train of Spirit impressions and revelatory knowing that allowed me to minister to them sweet words of edification they needed to hear from their Lord. Often I would see images or pictures. Sometimes I would feel an ache in my body where they had a disease.

God can speak softly but he carries a big stick. I have had discerning words from the Lord come to me that ministered deep heart-felt deliverance, all the while sitting quietly at a coffee shop across the table from a troubled soul who got healed in that moment. God's grace came. Truth expelled darkness. The devil's lie was undone. Their marriage was saved. Volume has nothing to do with authority. God offers a lifeline. His words penetrate.

Ordinary prophecy in the church today is not about predicting the future. More about that later. Prophesying is a wonderful gift of God that is intended to operate within a gathering of Christians. It can also be extremely useful in evangelizing strangers. In church it has a clearly defined purpose, to edify (build up), to exhort (encourage) and to console (comfort). Here are the boundaries for the content of prophetic words…. *But one who prophesies speaks to men for edification and exhortation and consolation. One who speaks in a tongue edifies himself; but one who prophesies edifies the church.* (1 Cor 14:3-4) There are times in our life when the thing we need the most is to hear a word from the Lord that speaks to us right where we are. Prophecy does that.

Prophesying by the Spirit (a spontaneously spoken word) is always about building up believers in their faith, pointing people to Christ, encouraging their faith, and activating spiritual gifts or ministries within the body. *Let all things be done for edification.* (1 Cor 14:26) *But all things must be done properly and in an orderly manner.* (1 Cor 14:40) God upholds decency and decorum. There are limits put around the use of gifts to safeguard them, especially tongues and prophecy. They impact God's people powerfully. Prophecy never shames, exposes, or condemns a sincere believer. Real prophecy is safe.

SIGNS AND WONDERS

IF YOU ARE GOING down a highway and become lost, you need to see a sign. A sign can save your life. "Gas five miles ahead." "Turn right on highway 45." "Slow down. Bridge out." Natural signs happen all around us. Signs are meant to grab attention. They interrupt the usual flow. We ought to know the signs of the times; discern the seasons.

Scripturally, signs refer to a supernatural attestation of God's presence. They indicate that the word of the Lord being declared or being taught is true, so pay attention. Signs are observable indicators or noticeable marks that heaven is breaking in on our earthly realm. Frequently I have preached or taught then afterwards I've said, *"Let's see what the Holy Spirit wants to do now."* I expect confirming signs from God. I'll lead my audience to wait expectantly for the Lord to confirm his word. This is always edifying and often surprising.

Signs are the dinner bell for the gospel. In countries where open preaching of the gospel is rare, the Lord may use dramatic public miracles to cause people to gather, listen, and be saved. The blind see, the deaf hear, the lame walk. "Come and see!" Signs may be seen when a demonic strongman over a region is pulled down, or idolatry's deception is exposed. The gospel shakes the foundation of dark powers. Mass conversions may follow.

Jesus said signs should follow his believers. *These signs will accompany those who have believed: in My name they will cast out demons, they will speak with new tongues...* Mark 16:17

The presence of supernatural signs such as deliverance or new tongues is not uncommon. Nor is it unbiblical. Jesus said to expect it. On the day of Pentecost, Peter pointed out some things that the people had seen or had heard as the Spirit came. He said these attesting signs confirmed God's word as true.

...having received from the Father the promise of the Holy Spirit, He has poured forth this which you both see and hear... (Acts 2:33) What was it they had just seen or heard? They had seen and heard people speaking in unknown tongues. It is a secret source of power. Perhaps no other gift is hated more by Satan than this little gift. He certainly fights against Christians discovering it or using it. Peter defended it as he quoted the prophet Joel to explain that this sign was God's word being fulfilled.

"Even on MY bondslaves, both men and women, I will in those days pour forth of MY Spirit And they shall prophesy." Acts 2:18 NAS (quoting Joel 2)

Some signs are less obvious but should always be present in individual believers, such as the fruit of the Spirit. *But the fruit of the Spirit is love, joy, peace, patience, kindness, goodness, faithfulness, gentleness, self-control...* (Gal 5:22-23). The character of Christ is worked into us.

Another set of signs among Christians as a whole are the distinctives of being in his kingdom. *...for the kingdom of God is not eating and drinking, but righteousness and peace and joy in the Holy Spirit.* (Rom 14:17) These are the relational signs of being in covenant community.

My favorite overt signs are immediate manifest miracles, sometimes startling, that dramatically confirm the preaching of God's word. Of course, the greatest miracle of all is the new birth! People becoming saved is a miracle.

While I was doing the work of an evangelist, I saw the lame walk and the deaf hear. We need to know that God's word is true and is authentic. Jesus said we could expect this to happen. *And they went out and preached everywhere, while the Lord worked with them, and confirmed the word by the signs that followed. (Mark 16:20)* The followers of Christ were bold in proclaiming the resurrection of Jesus. Why? Because God backed them up with signs, wonders, and miracles.

Those hearing the gospel, perhaps for the very first time, need a boost. People need to know that Jesus is alive, risen from the grave. We all need to be able to put faith and full reliance on the word of God. We need to know that God is alive. Signs help us do that. Another way signs can assist us is by confirming that the messenger is someone sent by God, that they are authorized, and that we should pay attention to them. Paul said this about his own ministry. *The signs of a true apostle were performed among you with all perseverance, by signs and wonders and miracles.* 2 Cor. 12:11

God gives credentials to his chosen servants, especially when they are on an assignment combating evil spiritual forces. We wear a badge. This often happens to evangelists or apostles. Any believer can have their word attested to by signs. Prophets also have confirming signs. One sign that commonly follows my ministry is that people easily receive the gift of the Holy Spirit by the laying on of my hands after I have preached the word.

Jesus said to the Jews that if they didn't believe his word (which most weren't receiving) they should at least listen to him because of the works (*i.e.*- signs and wonders) that the Father was performing through him. *...the works which the Father has given Me to accomplish—the very works that I do—testify about Me, that the Father has sent Me.* John 5:36

Peter declared that the signs Jesus performed attested to the fact that God sent Jesus. *Men of Israel, listen to these words: Jesus the Nazarene, a man attested to you by God with miracles and wonders and signs which God performed through Him in your midst, just as you yourselves know*— (Acts 2:22) Because of these miracles, their sin by rejecting Jesus was even greater.

Can signs deceive you? Yes. That's why we need to know the written word and we need to be taught by trained teachers. The presence of counterfeit signs is another reason why we need genuine signs. We need to be able to say, "This is real" or, "That is false." Looking for a sign can lead you in the right direction, *if* it is a sign from God, and *if* your heart is sincere. False signs do deceive gullible people. Good signs encourage the faithful. Remember, the gift of prophecy being on display is a sign from God.

Jesus warned about deception in Mark 13:22. *...false prophets will arise, and will show signs and wonders, in order to lead astray, if possible, the elect. But take heed; behold, I have told you everything in advance.* The danger of being deceived is a grave risk in the last days. Knowing God's word can save us. False signs come from false prophets. They don't preach Jesus. They deny the incarnation. The refute the gospel. They are corrupt liars.

Prophets (*i.e.*- godly, genuine, anointed men or women) often have accompanying signs. For example, God shows them things. Their words come true. They may have dreams and visions. They receive words of knowledge. The secrets of men's hearts are revealed. Sometimes they see the future. They have peculiar insight into the things of the Sprit and God's word. Genuine prophets of the Lord usually have a considerable amount of spiritual grace accompanying their ministry. They stir things up and break open new biblical truth. Prophets are anointed by the Holy Spirit. Prophets often prophesy therefore, signs follow them. Prophesying is itself a sign that heaven is breaking through into our world.

The fact that false prophets exist doesn't do away with real prophets. False signs and false prophets lead people astray. Good signs and good prophets lead people to salvation. *Then I fell at his feet to worship him. But he *said to me, "Do not do that; I am a fellow servant of yours and your brethren who hold the testimony of Jesus; worship God. For the testimony of Jesus is the spirit of prophecy."* (Rev 19:10-11) Jesus is front and center. Pure prophecy points to and promotes Jesus. Prophecy always exalts Jesus Christ and testifies to his reality. Angels show up when prophecy erupts. Hey, Jesus is alive! Real prophecy always stays in agreement with the scriptures.

Our safety to avoid error is to know the scriptures and to have a love for the truth. Genuine signs point toward God, help people believe in Jesus, and verify the truth of God's word. Signs are what first caused Jesus' new followers to begin putting their faith in him. *This beginning of His signs Jesus did in Cana of Galilee, and manifested His glory, and His disciples believed in Him.* (John 2:11) Signs can help us believe God's word.

God uses signs and wonders to get our attention. Human nature is alert to things out of the ordinary, things that stand out. Signs are indicators of danger or of opportunity. The scriptures admit this. *For indeed Jews ask for signs and Greeks search for wisdom; but we preach Christ crucified...* (1 Cor. 14:22) Some Jews had come to Jesus and asked to see a sign from him. (Mt. 12:38) In this case, their request was evidence of disbelief, an insincere test. "If you are the Messiah, prove it!" They looked for an excuse to disqualify him. Jesus did not grant their request. He said to the stubborn Jews with hardened hearts that no sign would be given to them except the sign of Jonah in the whale - his resurrection after three days. But sincere seekers like the Roman Centurion with the sick servant got a miracle. (Matthew 8:5-13) Real faith receives a real reward.

The writer of Hebrews explained that God can communicate through signs. Signs are attesting miracles. *God also testifying with them, both by signs and wonders and by various miracles and by gifts of the Holy Spirit according to His own will.* (Heb. 2:4) Notice, these accompanying displays of power or of revelation go along with our testimony, preaching, or proclamation. It can be a partnership with God. This happened in both the Old and New Testament eras. God bears witness (i.e.- he testifies) along with us, especially when it is a prophet that is speaking. The absence of signs or gifts of the Spirit, or prophets disappearing from the church, is a sad reproach.

We do not see our signs;
There is no longer any prophet,
Nor is there any among us who knows how long.
How long, O God, will the adversary revile,
And the enemy spurn Your name forever?

Psalms 74:9-10 KJV

Not only is the gift of prophecy a sign, but the presence of a prophet is a sign. The arrival of prophets can be a "plus sign" that God is about to upset the apple cart or turn the tables on his enemies. If prophets are absent, that's a sign, but it's negative. It is an indicator that God is not with us. We need to repent and seek Him.

Prophets discern times and seasons. Prophets disclose the tactics of the enemy. Prophets often declare significant events to help God's people. Signs are additional proof that the word declared is from God, evidence that we stood in his counsel. Our word has an additional witness – the Holy Spirit. Included among miraculous attestations are the gifts of the Holy Spirit. All the gifts, everyone one of them, are signs and wonders. All the gifts should prompt us to thank the Lord.

But to each one is given the manifestation of the Spirit for the common good. For to one is given the word of wisdom through the Spirit, and to another the word of knowledge according to the same Spirit; to another faith by the same Spirit, and to another gifts of healing by the one Spirit, and to another the effecting of miracles, and to another prophecy, and to another the distinguishing of spirits, to another various kinds of tongues, and to another the interpretation of tongues. But one and the same Spirit works all these things, distributing to each one individually just as He wills. 1 Cor 12:7-11

A sign is something originating outside of our space-time world. Signs are the breath of heaven blowing into our earthly room. A sign is the finger of God touching our dimension. Realize that in this universe we are limited to living in four dimensions: length, breadth, height, and time. There are more dimensions than these, we just are not aware of them. God is not bound by our universe. He is outside of space-time.

God is supernatural and he is spirit-being. This is another reason why Christians (corporately) should have all of the gifts of the Spirit – not just prophecy – routinely operating in their lives. The supernatural gifts of the Spirit are a necessary and normal sign that God is among us, that the God of heaven has not left us alone. The opposite of this, the absence of signs, should be of great concern among us. If we don't have them, there is a reason why.

PROPHECY SIGNALS BELIEVERS

WHEN THE FOLLOWERS OF Jesus assemble together, what things distinguish their meeting? Is it dead and dry like a civic club? What sets it apart? What can be expected to happen? What makes a gathering of believers different from a concert, a business meeting, a college lecture, or a birthday party? The answer? The manifest presence of God! God who is omnipresent becomes manifest. He who is a breath becomes a hand. God becomes tangible.

Jesus promised his followers that if they gathered in his name, he would be there. *For where two or three have gathered together in My name, I am there in their midst.* (Matt 18:20) The kingdom of God has come among us. Why? Because the King has arrived. His name is "God with us" or Immanuel.

Whenever I host a Christian meeting and the presence of the Lord appears or the Spirit's gifts are manifested, I say to the people, *"We should praise the Lord for his presence. Don't take this for granted. He didn't have to show up, you know!"* Always be thankful. Always acknowledge him and appreciate his presence. God likes to hang with those who love him.

When Jesus shows up, what can we expect to see? If the presence of God is what distinguishes a gathering of Christians from a secular gathering, then what are the marks of God's presence among us? Does the Lord make himself known? I say the one important distinguishing mark that God is indeed among us as his church (his *ecclesia*) is the visible, audible, primary evidentiary sign: we will hear the gift prophecy in operation. Prophecy is a sign to believers that the Risen Christ is among us.

So then tongues are for a sign, not to those who believe but to unbelievers; but prophecy is for a sign, not to unbelievers but to those who believe. 1 Cor 14:22

Therefore if the whole church assembles together and all speak in tongues, and ungifted men or unbelievers enter, will they not say that you are mad? But if all prophesy, and an unbeliever or an ungifted man enters, he is convicted by all, he is called to account by all; the secrets of his heart are disclosed; and so he will fall on his face and worship God, declaring that God is certainly among you. 1 Cor 14:20-26

The revelatory aspect of prophesying can uncover concealed secrets. If not to others, then to the one hearing it. You know that He knows! The Holy Spirit reveals the hidden things in people's hearts. His light penetrates. If a novice or untaught person is present among believers, they will know that God is among you.

Wouldn't you enjoy being among a group of Christians where secret sin can't be concealed? Where hypocrites repent? Where sinners get saved? I've seen it happen!

It is so strengthening to our faith when the Lord reveals his heart and mind to us by his Spirit. Prophecy does this for us. How would you feel if you were downcast and discouraged when you came in, but uplifted and stronger when you went out? You have to experience this in operation to truly appreciate it. Once you do, you'll appreciate it and rejoice. You'll never voluntarily forego being among believers where this gift freely happens.

This supernatural charismatic gift, the ability for ordinary believers to prophesy to one another, should be eagerly desired by us all. We need to minister prophetically to each other. This practice will transform our walk with God and elevate our mutual love as brothers and sisters in Christ to a much higher level. We become his living body, ready to minister, sharing his living word. We know that Christ is indeed among us when he speaks to us (or through us) by his Spirit. Your prayer life will go up a notch when you are always full of the Spirit; as you stay ready to speak any fresh word from the Lord.

TONGUES CONVINCE UNBELIEVERS

WHILE PROPHECY IS A SIGN to believers, unknown tongues serve as a sign to unbelievers. Both of these verbal gifts are by the Holy Spirit. They are supernatural, not a learned language. Either gift may be appropriate on certain occasions. If you've never heard a heavenly language or prayed in an unknown tongue, it may seem startling at first. I've been in meetings when an unbeliever heard an untaught Christian speak in Russian or in Latin. It shocked my skeptical friends. I've heard first-hand reports of Christians overseas speaking in a heavenly tongue, not knowing the local language, but a native heard him speaking in their words and it was an exhortation for them to turn to God. It's real. But most tongues of the Spirit are not directed toward men but to God.

Peter said the tongues people heard on the day of Pentecost were a sign to the mixed multitude, the crowd present in Jerusalem. People from many different nations heard untaught Christians speaking to them directly in their own languages. (See Acts 2) Many turned to God.

In the Law it is written, "BY men of strange tongues and by the lips of strangers I will speak to this people, and even so they will not listen to ME," says the Lord. So then tongues are for a sign, not to those who believe but to unbelievers; but prophecy is for a sign, not to unbelievers but to those who believe. (1 Cor 14:21) These signs were a convincing proof that God had now extended his word to all the nations, not just to the Hebrews. Now, all men everywhere were to repent to God and put their faith in Jesus. The gospel had gone global.

This use of tongues, as the Spirit wills, is a sign to unbelievers. I've seen this gift operate in my life as a sign to "unbelieving" believers too; that is, to someone who was struggling to believe.

In the first case, I was pastoring a Baptist church in Florida. The folks were unfamiliar with the gifts of the Spirit and were a bit fearful of them. I had a beloved deacon in the church who had hurt his back. He asked me to be praying for him. After several days, he was still in pain, almost unable to walk. I asked if I could come see him and pray directly for him in his home. He was stretched out on his belly on a couch in the den when I arrived. With his permission, I laid my hands on his back and began to pray. After a. minute, I felt a need for more power. I said, "Joey, would you mind if I prayed for you in my prayer language?" He looked up at me, grinned, and said, "Go ahead, pastor. We all know you do it." I went on quietly praying for him but this time in unknown tongues. By the next day he was fully healed.

Here is another testimony about tongues. A dear friend of mine called me with an urgent need for healing. He'd been battling a bad kidney problem. His grown son had been on dialysis and had a kidney transplant, so this may have run in the family. After many visits to the medical specialist, my friend David was scheduled for abdominal surgery to remove the kidney blockages. Both of his kidneys were filled with stones, some almost an inch in size. This was a frightening and painful prospect. They had already tried a lithotripsy procedure and laparoscopic surgery through his back. Both had failed. This next step was dreadful.

On the phone with David, I asked him if this time, would he mind if I prayed for him using my Spirit language? He agreed. I began to intercede for him in unknown tongues. He didn't understand a word I said. I didn't have any awareness of what my words meant either. I wasn't talking to David, I was talking to God, entreating him with all my heart. This went on about three minutes. The next day David went back to his surgeon for final x-rays before hospital admission the following day. In his office, the doctor took a long time looking at his new x-rays. He came back and told him to come with him down the hall. He showed him the x-rays on the light table and said, "What do you see?" David replied, "Nothing." The doctor said, "That's right. There's nothing there. The kidney stones have disappeared. I'm cancelling your surgery." As I write this, David is still healed today, several years later.

I believe praying in unknown tongues is a powerful form of prayer. It is a perfect prayer, exactly in line with the will of God. In both of these cases, praying in tongues produced divine intervention. It was a signal of God's great love and mercy to two believers who were struggling to exercise greater faith. Don't underestimate the power of praying in the Spirit.

Another use of unknown tongues is prominent in the emerging church. That is, the use of unknown tongues followed by the gift of interpretation. This makes the word intelligible to the hearers and thereby it is the equivalent of the gift of prophecy. Tongues plus interpretation (if it's meant to be interpreted) is equal to prophesying.

I believe some tongues in the church are a travailing prayer spoken to God, not to men. When that occurs, they are not meant to be interpreted. I also believe, based on my experiences, that a stand-alone message in unknown tongues may be a sign, a signal that's meant to get people to listen. Why is this needed? In too many gatherings, there is no room for the Spirit to speak. Everything is tightly programmed. God may decide to interrupt things with tongues to create a pregnant pause. What follows next is a prophetic utterance, not an interpretation of that tongue. Discernment is required. The point is, tongues are a sign to unbelievers that the Lord is present. Even Christians may need a sign if they have sunk down into unbelief. Tongues may glorify God with praise, or they can be powerful prayers in a heavenly language. They are not insignificant. They build you up. You need this. Tongues are a good sign from heaven. Listen up!

Now I wish that you all spoke in tongues, but even more that you would prophesy; and greater is one who prophesies than one who speaks in tongues, unless he interprets, so that the church may receive edifying. 1 Cor 14:5

This use of tongues is for everyone to exercise. It is for your own edification in private devotions or personal prayer. *For one who speaks in a tongue does not speak to men but to God; for no one understands, but in his spirit he speaks mysteries.* (1 Cor 14:2) Prayer is speaking to God. It doesn't need to be interpreted. It is not heard by men unless it is unintentional. I know holy angels listen to us as we pray in tongues.

Let me interject something about the mystery of speaking in tongues. Tongues are trans-rational. They are beyond what we can figure out. It is a spirit language, not a mental language. What language does your spirit speak? When I pray in tongues my mind is not in charge, my spirit is. The words don't originate in my mind from any vocabulary I have previously learned. I think one reason why the Lord uses this method of tongues for our personal edification is precisely because it humbles our mind. Praying in a heavenly language is for the humble and the hungry. Our proud mental powers, at this point, kneel down before the mystery of our holy God.

PRAYING IN TONGUES

PAUL SAID TONGUES WILL vary. I think this is in both their kind and in their usage. They can sound different and they can do different things. (1 Cor 12:10) He said God had appointed various kinds of tongues in the church. (1 Cor 12:28) Tongues don't all sound the same. Tongues are established in the church (*i.e.*- appointed). Therefore, since they are set in the church, they haven't gone away. They are still needed. In the church, the public use of tongues among the gathered saints is not for everyone. (1 Cor 12:30) Not all have this public gift. Yet Paul wanted everyone to be able to speak in tongues (1 Cor 14:5) and he said prophecy was more valuable in the meetings than unknown tongues. (1 Cor 14:5, 6) Paul also said he spoke in tongues more than all the Corinthians, which is saying a lot. (1 Cor 14:18) Overuse of tongues in the assembly can cause confusion. (1 Cor 14:23) Yet the church was not to prohibit speaking in tongues. (1 Cor

12:39) They key to understanding this is to know the difference between public and private usage of tongues.

The late Dr. Bill Bright of Campus Crusade for Christ had adopted a policy of "forbid not, encourage not." His main focus was winning souls. But he had many Spirit-filled students who were part of his enormous campus outreach. He made a wise decision that included everyone. Spirit-filled people should have grace to be cooperative and keep the main thing the main thing. None Spirit-filled folks should give us liberty to be ourselves as well.

Praying or worshipping in tongues is a privilege that I greatly enjoy. Speaking words by the Spirit for me began with speaking the language of angels (unknown tongues), then later I spoke words by the Spirit (prophesying in English). I had to learn how to get out of my head and speak from my heart - the place where the Spirit was dwelling. In my experience, unknown tongues and being able to prophesy are closely connected.

Let me explain how any believer can easily receive the gift of the Holy Spirit. This is important to know.

First, since all the gifts from God are received by faith, it's important for you to believe that God wants you to have this. This is not something you have to convince a reluctant Daddy to give you. It is his good pleasure to give you gifts, to give you all the good things of his kingdom.

Jesus had said the Holy Spirit would arrive. *Gathering them together, He commanded them not to leave Jerusalem, but to wait for what the Father had promised, "Which," He said, "you heard of from Me; for John baptized with water, but you will be baptized with the Holy Spirit not many days from now."* Acts 1:4-5

The words "baptized in the Spirit" are identical to the phrase describing what the prophet John had been doing. He had baptized people in water in the Jordan River. Just like his converts were dipped into water, Jesus' disciples would be dipped into Holy Spirit. The word *baptized* is a Greek word meaning dipped or immersed, like dipping a biscuit in gravy. When you're dipped in the water, it gets all over you. You are covered with it. To be technical about it, the Greek word in the text can mean "in, with, or by." All three are correct. People see the evidence. Baptism is messy. Once you've been baptized, you need a change of clothes.

The Holy Spirit is the promise of the Father. It was guaranteed by Jesus. He sent him (the Spirit) to us. He mentioned a change of clothes! Here are his words…

And behold, I am sending forth the promise of My Father upon you; but you are to stay in the city until you are clothed with power from on high. Luke 24:29

Let's suppose that you decide you truly desire this gift. You've studied the scriptures. You deliberately pursue it in prayer. You meet with some prayer partners who have already received it. You ask them to lay hands on you for this gift to be imparted. It happens like that very frequently. Or, you even can get alone with God and receive this gift by yourself. Either way is fine.

If you are seeking God by yourself, find a quiet place where you won't be interrupted. This will become your prayer room. I will explain the simple steps involved to receive this wonderful gift. It is all in the Bible in Acts 2.

When the day of Pentecost had come, they were all together in one place. And suddenly there came from heaven a noise like a violent rushing wind, and it filled the whole house where they were sitting. And there appeared to them tongues as of fire distributing themselves, and they rested on each one of them. And they were all filled with the Holy Spirit and began to speak with other tongues, as the Spirit was giving them utterance. (vs 2-4)

Notice what they were doing. They had all been spending time praying. Where were they? In an upper room, a private place set apart for prayer. They were seated, comfortable, waiting. A sequence of events occurred. They had to wait for a certain feast to fully arrive, the Day of Pentecost. For the Jews, this celebration had to be prophetically fulfilled. You and I don't need to wait for any certain time to arrive to receive this gift.

The next thing that happened is the wind of God blew into the room. I think it stormed in like hurricane! They sensed it and felt it. The room was alive with God's invisible electric presence. Discerning people can walk into a room and feel God's presence in the room.

The next thing that happened was flames of fire came and rested on each of them. Now, it was no longer just the room that was occupied by God, but each one of them was feeling God's physical anointing, something coming on them from above, his manifest presence on them, resting tangibly on each individual's body. When I feel this, it makes the hair stand up on my arms like electricity.

The next thing that happened was the Holy Spirit went down inside every one of them, filling them with his presence. God's presence wasn't only in the room. It wasn't only on their body. Now, his presence was inside them and filling them up. They were being filled with the Holy Spirit. What more could possibly occur?

The next thing that happened was they overflowed. They began to speak praises to God. What kind of language? It was unknown tongues. Another way to put this is, they spoke in conjunction with the Holy Spirit. They spoke as the Spirit gave them words to speak The Sprit was giving them utterance. Now there was something for onlookers to see and hear. In the upper room, no one doubted that the Christians had indeed received the gift of God, the Holy Spirit's fulness.

Think with me about the four distinct stages I've described in the verses above. Have you ever been praying when this began happening to you? How far did you let it go? If the Holy Spirit comes into a room, can you get up and leave? Yes, you can. You can end it there and say, "That was nice!"

Let's take it a step further. The Holy Spirit can rest directly on you and you can feel his divine energy touching you. You can stop the experience right there and say "Wow! That was wonderful! I felt his power!"

Let's assume you want more. You welcome the Holy Spirit inside you. You become a yielded vessel. This thrills you. You are basking in his love and peace and joy. You have faith that this is what you asked for. He is now giving it to you. He's filling you up. Take all you want! God's supply never runs out. Thank him for it. Can you stop there? Certainly. Go on your way filled with God.

Suppose that your encounter with God exceeds what your rational mind can express, that words can no longer describe what you are experiencing. Here is when you can choose to speak words, not that you know already or are thinking up, but words coming from your spirit having been filled with His Spirit, words that come from heaven, the language of angels.

You do the speaking (it is your mouth and tongue) but the Holy Spirit's breath in you supplies the words. You choose to speak but you now yield your tongue to your spirit. You begin using your prayer language. Your spirit is now joyously exalting God!

Don't be afraid to ask God for this sweet gift. He loves to pour out this blessing on his children. Don't be afraid that something bad will happen to you. If you're a blood-bought redeemed child of God, you are in a safe zone. God has promised not to disappoint you!

"So I say to you, ask, and it will be given to you; seek, and you will find; knock, and it will be opened to you. For everyone who asks, receives; and he who seeks, finds; and to him who knocks, it will be opened. Now suppose one of you fathers is asked by his son for a fish; he will not give him a snake instead of a fish, will he? Or if he is asked for an egg, he will not give him a scorpion, will he? If you then, being evil, know how to give good gifts to your children, how much more will your heavenly Father give the Holy Spirit to those who ask Him?" Luke 11:9-13

This is the privilege of all believers, all the Spirit-filled charismatic Christians all over the world. A huge percentage of Jesus' follower are now living this way. Based on seeing these simple steps, I hope you find it easier now to ask the Lord to give you this wonderful gift, the baptism in the Holy Spirit.

WORSHIP IN THE SPIRIT

WHEN WE PRAY in a heavenly language, this is called worshipping in the Spirit. Your spirit is praising God, magnifying the Lord, giving thanks, sometimes with exuberant joy. This is when the altar of your heart is being set on fire with a sacrifice of praise. *...you also, as living stones, are being built up as a spiritual house for a holy priesthood, to offer up spiritual sacrifices acceptable to God through Jesus Christ.* 1 Pet 2:5

We are talking about prophesying in the Spirit, aren't we? It makes sense to me that if we want to prophesy fluently, we should be able to speak in unknown tongues. For this reason, we need the fountainhead of all the charismatic gifts, the baptism in the Holy Spirit. He fills us, then he overflows through us with his words.

I was gratified to learn recently that a British theologian whom I have followed for many years, N.T. Wright, speaks in tongues in his private devotions.

Professor Wright is the author of several of my favorite Christian resource books. He is an excellent teacher. I consider him (as do many) to be perhaps the world's foremost evangelical Bible scholar. His book, *Surprised by Hope,* is a landmark treatise on the resurrection of the saints. I was glad to hear him say that he is Spirit-filled.

There are a variety of heavenly tongues just like there are a variety of human languages. What language does God speak? Isn't it good to know that he can speak in a language you can know? You can speak in his language!

Angels speak in heavenly tongues. Paul said that his unknown tongues were of men *and* of angels. (1 Cor 13:1) Paul spoke in a spiritual language that angels recognized. Speaking in tongues is not a learned language but a supernatural grace. The amazing and dedicated group, Wycliffe Bible Translators, train workers to take the Bible to the remaining indigenous people groups of the earth that have not yet heard the gospel. But unknown tongues are not for preaching. They are used to speak to God in prayer, not to men. Don't forbid speaking in tongues lest you shut off the miracle you so desperately need.

PROPHECY IS NORMAL

PROPHECY IN THE MODERN church is a normal part of the revival in the last days. *'And it shall be in the last days,' God says, 'That I will pour forth of MY Spirit on all mankind; And your sons and your daughters shall prophesy...* (Acts 2:17)

Solid theological insight affirms that the gift of prophecy is biblical and is meant to operate in the modern church.[4] The phenomenon of prophesying attests that God is pouring out his Spirit on all of mankind. On the day of Pentecost this fulfillment of the Scriptures included the sign of unknown tongues. Prophesying by believers, even young people, is evidence that we are in the last days. This is occurring everywhere - except among some church populations that resist it. Most of the modern church is going through a transformation. God is leaping over religious barriers. The risen Christ is preparing the earth

---

[4] *The Gift of Prophecy,* Wayne Grudem, Crossway Books, 2000.

to receive his kingdom as the gospel is declared. Everybody everywhere is being affected by it. To me, this is an indicator that the world's harvest fields are ripening. We need to lift up our eyes and see it. More laborers need to be equipped. We need to go outside the sanctuary with the gospel. The Spirit is here to help us.

When the church moved away from its apostolic origin, it began to adopt pagan systems of order, accepting many false traditions and structures. Most of its doctrine remained intact but its ecclesiology, its beliefs about church practices and protocols, became corrupted.

This happened after the third century AD after the Roman Emporer Constantine made Christianity his official state religion.[5] The church left the houses of believers and moved into dedicated temples. Some saw this as keeping the pattern of the Old Testament, the order of priests. Those meetings centered on re-enacting the sacrifice of Christ through ministering the ritual of the bread and the wine, holy communion, the eucharist. Regardless, the ministry returned to a select few, a dedicated elite clergy. This left the body of believers behind. Gifts of the Spirit mostly dwindled, except for a remnant through the ages.

You can see this pattern formalized beautifully today in those branches of Christianity called "high church," where the meetings focus on liturgy and the priest serves the eucharist. Among Protestants, the focus has shifted

---

[5] *Pagan Christianity* by George Barna and Frank Viola, 2012, Tyndale House Publishers.

since the Reformation. In less formal churches, the focus of the Sunday meetings is on the preacher who delivers a sermon. The preacher and a choir are the center of everything, not the members. This is even true today among Spirit-filled or Pentecostal churches, except they usually have livelier singing. But gifts are rare.

The bottom line is this: the structure of large congregations who meet in religious facilities with a hierarchy of leaders and a rigid order of service *mitigates against* the free exercise of charismatic gifts by the body of believers. The gifts of believers don't work well in big meetings. Only the main speakers get to use their gifts. To the members sitting in the pews, it seems like we've programmed God out of the assembly.

If we removed the Holy Spirit from the church, nothing much would change. The ministers who lead most churches or denominations never give a thought to equipping the saints for the ministry or urging members to covet to prophesy. That activity might endanger their privileged roles as clergy.

I will note that there are some exceptions, mostly by individual Spirit-filled ministers, who as an evangelist, may carry a gift of healing; or by a few pastor-prophets who are urging renewal and stirring up the saints to seek the Lord. But even when they succeed in bringing revival, traditional structures still resist the new wine.

I should mention there are two major differences in the way that prophetic revelation flows. The Holy Spirit interacts with different people in different ways. Common threads exist but great variety occurs. The two major differences are whether a person being graced with the gift of prophecy either *sees* something or *says* something. The New Testament is filled with accounts of people who had dreams or saw visions. The Old Testament illustrates this.

In the Old Testament, some prophets were called seers. This means they had a high visionary capacity. God spoke to them through visual aids or vivid scenes. Their imagination or ability to see by the Spirit was strong. Elijah and Elisha were prophets who saw visions. Isaiah saw the Lord high and lifted up. Visions affected what they spoke. Their words to the people and their prayers to the Lord were heard.

When Elisha was under attack, he wanted his associate to see the angels of God surrounding them, so he prayed for him. Then the young assistant saw the angel armies too.

Now when the attendant of the man of God had risen early and gone out, behold, an army with horses and chariots was circling the city. And his servant said to him, "Alas, my master! What shall we do?" So he answered, "Do not fear, for those who are with us are more than those who are with them." Then Elisha prayed and said, "O Lord, I pray, open his eyes that he may see." And the Lord opened the servant's eyes and he saw; and behold, the mountain was full of horses and chariots of fire all around Elisha. 1 Kings 6:15-17

Samuel the prophet anointed David to be king. Samuel was called a seer. Nathan and Gad who served King David's adminstration as prophets fit this category as seers. It is interesting to me that a king needed prophets around him. May every national leader have intercessors and prophets surround them and undergird them, to help them to do the will of God. I believe every leader of a church, a business, or a nation ought to seek out those who know the mind of the Lord and listen to them.

Other prophets were not so much seers but they had an ability to have a "bubbling up" flow of words as a stream of language, like water flowing up from a spring. They could speak words from God, releasing a message from heaven's spirit-realm, words that didn't originate in their head or come their own thoughts. These words reveal the mind and heart of God.

Abraham was such as a prophet. He also saw visions. David was called a prophet. Because David was a singer and songwriter, I imagine that he was the kind of prophet who had words that flowed up from the Spirit of God.

SEER OR SAYER

THERE ARE MANY different types of prophets. Not all believers who are graced with the gift of prophecy will function in the same way. Not all five-fold prophets look alike or talk alike. Some are not even loud! Among Christians who feel a special calling to pray for the nation, there is a big percentage who are high level functioning prophets (or have a lot of prophetic grace). But in their role as prayer warriors (my mother was such a one), they do a lot more *praying* than they do *saying.* Like all ministers, but perhaps more than most, prophets pray. The gift of spiritual insight and anointed unction operates through them to travail for sinners to be saved, for leaders to be protected and anointed, and for God's hand to be on the nation. Prophets usually pray in tongues a lot. They speak mysteries. They prophecy in their prayer time, not to men, but they're speaking to angels, even giving them instructions, often not realizing they were doing it.[6]

---

[6] Intercessory prayer and Spirit inspired prophecy attracts holy angels. See my book *Heaven's Angel Army* on Amazon.com.

The Hebrew word for prophet that God used to describe Abraham was *nabi*. It means someone who is a mouthpiece for God. The word used to describe Daniel as a seer is *roeh,* meaning a vision or someone who sees visions. Perhaps being a seer is indicative for how a visionary prophet communicates with God. All those who were called seers were also spokesmen in behalf of God. Prophets see things and say things. They didn't speak on their own authority but spoke based on what God had shown them.

Formerly in Israel, when a man went to inquire of God, he used to say, "Come, and let us go to the seer"; for he who is called a prophet now was formerly called a seer. 1 Sam 9:9

The Old Testament is filled with stories and examples that are meant to be lessons for believers in the New Testament. We learn from Moses, Abraham, David, the nation of Israel, and the Hebrew prophets. The difference is that in the old covenant the Spirit of God would rest on only a few select men or women as prophets, whereas in the new covenant, the Holy Spirit has been poured out on all believers in Christ Jesus. There are still prophets today and all believers may occasionally prophesy. We need to learn valuable lessons from the Old Testament.

Now these things happened to them as an example, and they were written for our instruction, upon whom the ends of the ages have come. 1 Cor 10:11

There is one particular Old Testament passage that has a lot of information about how God regards his "seers" and his "sayers." It is found in Numbers 12:1-9. Let's take a look at it.

Then Miriam and Aaron spoke against Moses because of the Cushite woman whom he had married (for he had married a Cushite woman); and they said, "Has the Lord indeed spoken only through Moses? Has He not spoken through us as well?" And the Lord heard it. (Now the man Moses was very humble, more than any man who was on the face of the earth.) Suddenly the Lord said to Moses and Aaron and to Miriam, "You three come out to the tent of meeting." So the three of them came out. Then the Lord came down in a pillar of cloud and stood at the doorway of the tent, and He called Aaron and Miriam. When they had both come forward, He said,
"Hear now My words:
If there is a prophet among you,
I, the Lord, shall make Myself known to him in a vision.
I shall speak with him in a dream.
"Not so, with My servant Moses,
He is faithful in all My household;
With him I speak mouth to mouth,
Even openly, and not in dark sayings,
And he beholds the form of the Lord.
Why then were you not afraid
To speak against My servant, against Moses?"
So the anger of the Lord burned against them and He departed.

Here are the main points:

• Criticism had arisen regarding Moses due to jealousy.

• Moses was a very humble man, uniquely so.

• God confronted Aaron and Miriam for this divisive sin.

• God said he gave revelation to ordinary prophets through dark sayings, hard to understand puzzles, *i.e.*- dreams and visions, but to Moses he spoke plainly, _face to face_ (Lit. *"mouth to mouth."*

Moses saw the form of God and heard God's words openly and clearly. Therefore, Aaron and Miriam should have feared God because of this, respected Moses above themselves, and not been critical of him. Their conduct had angered God.

HUMILITY IS IMPORTANT

I WOULD LIKE TO make an observation about Moses. He did not defend himself when he was criticized. He wasn't self-serving or arrogant. He didn't feel threatened. Moses was humble, meek, the meekest man on earth. Yet he had the greatest revelation of who God was and the greatest information from God for humanity of anyone on the earth. There is a connection between Moses' humility and his unusual ability to be with God and to receive great revelation. Can this be an important lesson for us today? I think so. Humility is not a very common trait among human beings, not even among Christians, not even among church leaders. This is probably why we receive so little revelation from God.

Religious people can become proud but sinners may quickly repent. God can easily deal with sin since Jesus is a very good Savior. But pride isn't easy to fix. Pride makes us stubborn. It resists God. It repels grace. It is incompatible with God. And the worst thing about pride?

You don't know you've got it! It's like bad breath. Others smell it on you, but you can't. To God's sensibilities, pride is like bad breath. He doesn't want to be close to it.

Why do I think pride is so poisonous? Because pride leads to independence, to separation from God. It's the opposite of humility. People who permit pride to be in their lives become dull to the Spirit. It causes distance toward God and erects a barrier. Pride is dangerous because it will mislead you. You will keep going when you should stop. Pride blinds you. I know about pride because it has tripped me up and snared me very often.

I think pride is my besetting sin. I confess that I've seen this sin in myself. I repent of it. I'm now to the place in my life where I choose to preemptively humble myself in advance before God calls me out or corrects me. I recall praying before a Sunday service at my church in West Virginia. This was years ago. Suddenly I saw a spiritual vision. I saw the scene from Isaiah chapter six where the prophet saw the Lord's throne and angels crying out, "Holy! Holy! Holy!" Deeply moved, I began saying, "God, you are so holy!" Immediately I heard him say, "Yes and I'm humble too." I was driven to my knees as I realized he was showing me something about myself. I repented. I wasn't like him. I wasn't humble. I do want to be like him. I want to commune with him.

I've come to realize that God is humble. That's his nature, just like he is holy. He doesn't think more highly of himself than he should. This happens to us whenever we get a taste of power or revelation. God knows everything and has all power, yet he doesn't boast. We learn a little and we get puffed up. We get a prophecy and feel on top of the mountain. We get a person healed and we're the top dog. No - it is all by grace! This easily happens to us if we are religious. We compare ourselves to sinners and think we're doing pretty good. Rare indeed is the individual who sees a lot by inspiration, yet stays meek, humble, and avoids self-promotion. Great revelation always brings with it great temptation. *"Love builds up, but knowledge puffs up."* The fact is, God resists the proud but gives more grace to the humble. If you want to see more by the Spirit you need to make a choice to humble yourself. It's an ongoing decision. Then once you see more revelation, stay even more humble still.

You younger men, likewise, be subject to your elders; and all of you, clothe yourselves with humility toward one another, for God is opposed to the proud, but gives grace to the humble. Therefore humble yourselves under the mighty hand of God, that He may exalt you at the proper time... 1 Peter 5:5-6

God's hand is mighty. You and I? We are not mighty. We are mortal and weak. God gives more grace to the humble. Are you humble? Then you are a candidate for greater grace. God opposes the proud. Are you proud? Then you will discover that God will push back against you. Why is this so? Because God is humble. He is incompatible with pride. But he enjoys being around people who are meek. For this reason, God liked Moses. Likewise, Christ Jesus is meek. Jesus rewards the humble. He said the meek would inherit the earth. Jesus is not pushy or arrogant. He knows how to yield, to surrender his will, how to serve others. The nature of God manifest in the flesh was Jesus – it was love – but it was also meekness. He was an obedient servant who went all the way, even to death on a humiliating cross.

When Paul was discussing his authority as an apostle, he put it like this: *Now I, Paul, myself urge you by **the meekness and gentleness of Christ—I who am meek** when face to face with you, but bold toward you when absent! I ask that when I am present I need not be bold with the confidence with which I propose to be courageous against some, who regard us as if we walked according to the flesh.* 2 Cor 10:1-3

He was contrasting the flesh with Christ's meekness. Jesus – nor any of his genuine apostles – ever try to lord it over people using carnal kinds of authority. Jesus himself said that his yoke was easy and his burden was light. *Come to Me, all who are weary and heavy-laden, and I will give you rest. Take My yoke upon you and learn from Me, for I am gentle and humble in heart, and you will find rest for your souls. For My yoke is easy and My burden is light."* (Matt 11:28-30) He doesn't crush our soul. He doesn't put us down.

If you mistakenly think that humility is weakness, you are wrong. Your thinking is badly distorted by the spirit of this age. Humility is not weakness but rather it is strength that has been yoked. It is power put under discipline. It is relying on God. God told the apostle Paul that his grace comes readily to the weak.

Because of the surpassing greatness of the revelations, for this reason, to keep me from exalting myself, there was given me a thorn in the flesh, a messenger of Satan to torment me—to keep me from exalting myself! Concerning this I implored the Lord three times that it might leave me. And He has said to me, "My grace is sufficient for you, for power is perfected in weakness." Most gladly, therefore, I will rather boast about my weaknesses, so that the power of Christ may dwell in me. Therefore I am well content with weaknesses, with insults, with distresses, with persecutions, with difficulties, for Christ's sake; for when I am weak, then I am strong. 2 Cor 12:1-9 NAS

Dreams, visions, and words from the Lord should never make you feel haughty or proud, as though you were somehow more worthy than others to be a chosen channel of God's revelation. Revelation is always by grace, not merit. Remember, God can speak through a lowly donkey or he can prophesy through a child. Charismatic giftings are not an occasion for you to be puffed up. Be pure of heart by being like Jesus. Stay humble. Be correctible. Be teachable. Listen to others. Be willing to admit your mistakes. Don't get a big head. Get down off your high horse. Stay low where it is safe. Honor others above yourself. Don't let your title make you feel entitled. Let God defend you and your words. Don't mix proud flesh with gifts of grace. Doing so will surely destroy you.

WORDS OF KNOWLEDGE

PROPHECY MAY INCLUDE words of knowledge. These are usually tidbits of divine information about a person's past or present. If it is a word of wisdom, it may help prepare for what's ahead. The purpose of such prophetic words is to exhort or comfort. The prophecy has more credibility because it addresses a thing that only that person knows about, secrets known only to God.

For to one is given the word of wisdom through the Spirit, and to another the word of knowledge according to the same Spirit.... 1 Cor 12:9

Notice also that it is a "word" of knowledge. That means it is a fragmentary piece of information, it is partial. But it's enough to let you (the hearer or recipient) realize that God knows the whole story. God knows a whole lot about us that he never discloses. Isn't that good news?

When a prophecy with words of knowledge is given to you, the affect is usually profound. You feel like you're being read like an open book! It seems that your whole life is being laid bare. I believe that when the spirit of prophecy is actively at work, it has an effect on the speaker *and* on the hearer. Both will feel it. The speaker is seeing something and by faith saying it, but the recipient is being uncovered and touched by the hand of God also.

For instance, when Jesus spoke to the woman at the well, he said that she had had five husbands. This was just a snippet of information that he would've had no way of knowing if the Holy Spirit hadn't shown it to him. But when she went back to the village and reported she'd seen the Messiah, she told them that he told her *everything* about her life!

So the woman left her waterpot, and went into the city and *said to the men, "Come, see a man who told me all the things that I have done; this is not the Christ, is it?" John 4:28

This is like the instance when God spoke to Hagar, the servant to Sara, who had fled. The Lord sent his angel to speak to her so she would have courage to return. When she heard this word, Hagar said, *"You are a God who sees."* (Gen 16:13) When God looks into our heart and prophesies to us or repeats part of our story line back to us, we realize that he has been watching us all along even when we struggled and felt abandoned or alone. Hagar felt like the Lord had been seeing everything.

For the word of God is alive and powerful. It is sharper than the sharpest two-edged sword, cutting between soul and spirit, between joint and marrow. It exposes our innermost thoughts and desires. Nothing in all creation is hidden from God. Everything is naked and exposed before his eyes, and he is the one to whom we are accountable. Hebrews 10:12-13 NLT

Words of knowledge are an aspect of prophetic revelation. This is distinct among charismatic grace-gifts. This gift can operate as a stand-alone anointing, an unveiling of data points, a sudden knowing of information that had been concealed. Or it can be words within a flow of other prophetic utterances. It is the Holy Spirit who is doing this. It has nothing to do with fortune-tellers or witchcraft. That stuff is evil and sinful. This is a flow of information that comes from the heart of your loving Lord.

I've had the Lord repeat back to me (via prophecy) a private conversation word for word, something the prophet could not have possibly overheard. It amazed me and startled me. It reassured me that God was watching me and listening to me.

A VIVID ILLUSTRATION

TO ILLUSTRATE HOW a word of knowledge can impact a person, let me choose a story about how this kind of prophetic ministry is beneficial. I was ministering for a Baptist pastor in Texas, explaining to his congregation how the gift of prophecy works.

When I finished speaking from the Bible, he asked me if I would minister by the Spirit to his people. Sometimes I just preach or teach the word; other times I demonstrate spiritual gifts, as God wills. I have no explanation for this except perhaps God knows the timing of things better than me. In that church, they had been praying for God to instruct them about his gifts. That's why I was sent there. The Lord performed some amazing signs that showed them proof of his presence that morning. My job was to be faithful to do what he was showing me to do.

Anyway, the pastor invited all those in the church who wanted to receive prophetic ministry to come line up across the front. About twenty-five people responded. I passed down the line praying for everyone, pausing and listening for what the Lord might say. I was speaking by the prompting of the Spirit, saying different encouraging words. It was prophetic edification for sure, but it was nothing special, just plain vanilla.

Then I came to a young married woman. All of a sudden, as she stood in front of me, words of knowledge with great authority sprang from my mouth: *"The Lord wants you to know that what happened to your parents will never happen to you!"*

I was as shocked as she was. I was hearing those words for the first time as they came out of my mouth, having no forethought or knowledge about what I was saying or what they meant. Words of knowledge, when delivered as a Spirit-inspired prophecy, are based on what God knows not on what the speaker knows. The words came up from my spirit, not my intellect or mind. I hadn't thought of them first. They surprised me.

She immediately raised her hands and began praising the Lord. She had tears of joy streaming down her face as she leaped up and down. The whole church was powerfully impacted by witnessing this. I didn't have a clue what was going on. Reverential awe of the Lord came upon those who knew her.

Afterwards, the pastor took me to lunch.

"Did you know anything about that young woman before you spoke to her?" he asked.

"No, I'd never met her," I replied.

The pastor knew her well. He went on to tell me her story. In the home in which she had been raised, both of her parents had divorced then married again, doing this repeatedly, three times. It was family chaos. Total instability. When it came time for this young woman to prepare for her own marriage she came to her pastor for counselling. She was very afraid, reluctant to be married, fearful that the same horrible thing would happen to her and her new husband as had happened to her parents.

Can you imagine the strong comfort she took from hearing this prophetic word? God is good. He is a God who sees us. He wanted her heart to be unafraid. It is very reassuring when we have fresh evidence of his great love.

By the way, this young lady had been crying out to the Lord in prayer for help. She wanted God's grace to overcome the sad history of her family life. Why was she the one who got the remarkable word? I have found that in many different situations the Lord remains silent whenever people just want a charismatic toy to play with, a proof that God speaks. God doesn't put on a demonstration for anyone. But when people are humbling their souls and praying, seeking his face, the Lord is ready, eager, and willing to answer them. He goes out of his way to show mercy to the tender-hearted. In such cases as that, it feels like people are pulling a word out of me, even if I had felt reluctant to step out. God meets the desperate and the hungry where they are. But hard-hearted, self-righteous religious hypocrites go away empty.

FUTURE WORDS

ONE THING YOU CAN always say about prophecies regarding the future is, "Time will tell." If you wait long enough, you'll find out whether the word was true or not. Of course, there were some prophecies that required centuries of waiting.

As to this salvation, the prophets who prophesied of the grace that would come to you made careful searches and inquiries, seeking to know what person or time the Spirit of Christ within them was indicating as He predicted the sufferings of Christ and the glories to follow. It was revealed to them that they were not serving themselves, but you, in these things which now have been announced to you through those who preached the gospel to you by the Holy Spirit sent from heaven—things into which angels long to look. 1 Peter 1:10-12

Several points are worth noting in this passage. Notice that it was prophets who prophesied. They predicted God's actions in human history. Prophets are distinct among the ministry offices. They are special. *"Touch not mine anointed and do my prophets no harm."* Psalms 105:15 KJV

Ordinary preachers don't predict the future, except they can say that if you die without Jesus, you'll die in your sins. Prophets are known for seeing or saying things by the Spirit. Prophecy calls people who are straying back to God's covenant. The prophetic writings in the Old Testament were for future generations. Prophets may reveal precise events yet to occur. Notice that God's prophets make careful searches or inquiries. They seek God for answers. They work hard at their task to fulfill their calling. They wait on the Lord to show them heavenly mysteries. They desire to know about Christ and salvation. The Spirit of Christ is the source of their inspiration and motivation. They get curious. They dig into the Scriptures so they can understand and share what God is showing them.

Prophetic revelation must move from mystical visions into the context of biblical history, insight, and understanding. Prophecy may sometimes predict the future, but the main thrust of ordinary prophecy today is to edify. In the church, genuine prophetic ministry does not ordinarily expose people's sins, shame them, condemn them, put them down, or embarrass them. A prophetic minister may see their sin, but a mature prophet will hide it from onlookers and instead speak words that minister grace, display mercy, and lead the recipient to repentance and restoration.

This protocol is true 99% of the time. Leave exceptions to seasoned prophets or mature apostles in those rare life and death situations, occasions where the Lord has had enough, or when someone is destroying the church. This happened to me as I was with a team of ministers trying to help a struggling church on Florida's east coast. The first day, we interviewed members and dialogued with the pastor and his wife. I saw something by the Spirit that the pastor hadn't told us. It was so startling I couldn't believe what I was seeing. Later, sin was confessed. The pastor and his wife were fighting each other for control of the church! Demons were active, jealousy was thick, pride was nauseous. The couple would not repent. The church soon disintegrated.

But one who prophesies speaks to men for edification and exhortation and consolation. One who speaks in a tongue edifies himself; but one who prophesies edifies the church. Now I wish that you all spoke in tongues, but even more that you would prophesy; and greater is one who prophesies than one who speaks in tongues, unless he interprets, so that the church may receive edifying. (1 Cor. 14:3-5).

When you hear someone speak a word that addresses the future, it is less common. In fact, it is rare. This reminds me that there are two kinds of future oriented words. One kind is sovereign, where the Lord is disclosing what he is going to do regardless of what we do. *"As surely as I live, saith the Lord..."*

The other kind of predictive prophetic word is like a promissory note. We can get in on it *if* we follow him fully. This word has to be redeemed or cashed in. *"If you will, then I will..."* It's a prophetic word describing a possible or probable outcome, but it's conditional based on our full faith and our complete obedience.

I've seen visions or dreams and I've spoken words that were predictive, but I can count them on one hand. Most prophetic words I've spoken in my ministry are for people needing hope, faith, or encouragement. In my experience, if someone frequently sees things that are in the future, that person has likely moved into a higher level from merely having a charismatic gift to prophesy. They may be becoming a prophet. Their grace level – its accuracy, faith, or revelation – is rising.

Not everyone who prophesies is a prophet. All believers may prophesy by the Spirit but only a few are in the office of a prophet. The ministry of a prophet is a high calling. It is among the fivefold ministries given to the church by the ascended Lord Jesus. (Eph 4:11-12) It is among those office gifts Christ has set into the church (1 Cor 12:28). Prophets are part of the foundation gifts that uphold the church, along with Christ Jesus, the chief cornerstone. (Eph 2:20) Warning: Do not call yourself into the office of a prophet! They go through grueling trials and ordeals. They get refined. The word they carry gets tested. You don't want to volunteer for this role unless you are drafted. *As an example, brethren, of suffering and patience, take the prophets who spoke in the name of the Lord.* James 5:10

Are real prophets (not just those who occasionally prophesy) a major part of the church? Yes, they are. Let's examine a key passage of scripture.

So then you are no longer strangers and aliens, but you are fellow citizens with the saints, and are of God's household, having been built on the foundation of the apostles and prophets, Christ Jesus Himself being the corner stone, in whom the whole building, being fitted together, is growing into a holy temple in the Lord, in whom you also are being built together into a dwelling of God in the Spirit. Eph 2:19-23

According to this scripture, the church's foundation includes apostles *and* prophets. They support weight in his holy temple. There are two ways of looking at this truth. The first is, we are established on the truth of the writings of the Old Testament prophets and the writings of the New Testament apostles. This is certainly valid. However, I believe there is more to it. The way of thinking prominent among evangelicals is that prophets are extinct, the era of apostles has ended, and the gifts of the Spirit have ceased. If this is true, then that leaves us with only the sacred scriptures, the Holy Bible, and the Holy Spirit. Thank God for the written word of God. I am not belittling that at all. However, another factor needs to be considered- *prophets.*

The head of the church, Jesus, is still calling, appointing, and sending prophets into the church. Jesus is the corner stone, but prophets are part of the church's foundation. This verse says his living temple is being fitted together. Ask yourself, do prophets fit into your church? Are they recognized for their role? Paul said the church was built together. Are prophets being built into your church? Are you connecting with contemporary prophets? Or is yours a non-prophet church?

This is what the key verse and its context in Ephesians 4:11 means. In that passage, Paul is saying that the Lord Jesus *from heaven* (after His ascension) is sending these ministers (apostles, prophets, etc.) to the church *on earth.* These key ministers are still being appointed by Jesus! This role of Christ has not changed. He is the same- *"yesterday today and forever."*

There is nothing wrong with recognizing the inspired words of prophets and apostles in the Bible. I devour the Bible. I love it! We need to hide God's word in our heart. His word keeps us. Love the Bible but honor and receive God's gifts to the church - the *persons* who are prophets.

By the way, not every word in the Scriptures was written by prophets or apostles. It's God's inspired word regardless of who penned it. Luke wrote the Gospel of Luke and he also wrote the Book of Acts. Yet he was not an apostle. He accompanied Paul on his travels and documented everything. Revere the Bible, believe it, adhere to it, but the church's foundation is more than a book. It is Jesus and his apostles and prophets.

The letter to the Ephesians gives us insight into the human foundation of the church. It is first a Person, the Lord Jesus Christ. Everything is built on him (and is being built by him). He is the Chief Cornerstone of the church. In other words, everything lines up with Him. He is also the plumb-line. If the temple doesn't line up with Jesus, then it's out of alignment. If his body doesn't connect with the head, we are disjointed, decapitated, lifeless.

But besides Jesus himself, God has given the church persons who are like the flooring that keeps us stable, his five-fold ministries. Among them are two major representatives that remind us of Jesus. These are God-called people, his apostles and prophets. I believe their grace to function increases when they work together. These ministers are contemporary gifts to the church, not just historic servants of God whose writings we still study. Paul stated this in the following passage of scripture.

By referring to this, when you read you can understand my insight into the mystery of Christ, which in other generations was not made known to the sons of men, as it has now been revealed to His holy apostles and prophets in the Spirit; Eph 3:4-5 Notice the word "now." Paul was saying that in his present day, now, after Jesus had ascended to heaven, there were people who were apostles and prophets learning about God's unfolding purpose. It wasn't only from ancient sacred writings. This remains true for us today. When God needs more apostles or prophets, he calls them, prepares them, and sends them to the church in every generation and to every nation.

If God has appointed prophets in the church, and if Jesus is still sending them to the church, wouldn't it be wise for us to recognize them and receive them? We need them for a number of reasons. I believe one vital role that prophets have in the modern church is teaching about the ministry of the Spirit and activating prophetic gifts among the members of the church. We still need prophets and we still need the gift of prophecy. We also need teachers to explain how all of this operates within the body of Christ.

HEARING FROM GOD

BACK TO THE IDEA of prophecy being a common charismatic gift. One factor I've been emphasizing is the benefit to receiving the Spirit's prophetic grace in your life, even if you are not able to meet with other Christians or able to share prophetic words. You don't need to have a platform, stage, church building, a title, or be behind a podium in order to prophesy. In fact, you don't need to be ordained, have a seminary degree, or be a full-time preacher or part time pastor. In fact, you don't even need an audience. You can prophesy to yourself! I have had the Lord do that very thing for me, especially when I was fasting and praying and needing fresh direction. Usually it came through an unknown tongue that I interpreted it. It was a personal prophecy for me.

Prophesying to yourself is a little bit like being a doctor and practicing medicine on your own body. It may not be the wisest thing to do. But it can be done. But do know the boundaries.

Why is this possible? Because prophesying is more about hearing *from* God than it is about speaking words *for* God to someone else. Let me repeat that: **The essence of prophecy is hearing from God**, not speaking for God. *"It is written, 'Man shall not live on bread alone, but on every word that proceeds out of the mouth of God.'"* Matt. 4:4 The Lord offers us a *proceeding word.*

Jesus is our Chief Shepherd. (*i.e.*- chief pastor, the Pastor of pastors) Christians are his sheep. We're in his flock. Jesus said, *"...the sheep hear his voice, and he calls his own sheep by name and leads them out. When he puts forth all his own, he goes ahead of them, and the sheep follow him because they know his voice.* John 10:3-4

Most people who are prophetic will hear a lot more than what they will ever say. A lot of times what we hear is meant to lead us to pray. It isn't meant for public consumption. Not every insight is designed to be revealed. We shouldn't blurt out what we hear all the time. *"Even a fool when he keeps silent may be considered wise."* There is a proper time to speak up. We should hold our peace until then. Practice hearing from God. The correct timing of speaking for God will then take care of itself.

The Lord wants to prophesy to you. Your heavenly Father desires to speak life into your dreams, hope into your heart, faith into you soul. God's life-giving word is flowing toward you! Our Lord Jesus is the Alpha and Omega, the beginning and the end. He will never leave you nor forsake you. Jesus has ascended into heaven where he is beyond time. He sees every bit of your timeline, your past, present, and future. He stands at the end of your destiny. From that finish line, he speaks words into your present that call you forward into your greatest fulfillment and rewards.

I dealt with the subject of *Hearing God's Voice* in a previous book with that same title. I'm grateful that biblical scholars like professor Jack Deere have written extensively about this topic.[7] We need to know that it is safe, biblical, and sane to experience hearing God's voice. As the Late Francis Shaeffer famously said, *"He is there, and He is not silent."*

---

[7] *Surprised by the Voice of God*, Jack Deere, Zondervan Publishing House, 1996.

STIFLING THE SPIRIT

PEOPLE HAVE A mistaken notion, that when God speaks through a person, the human vessel has no part in it. They think that God takes over and the person (or their mouth) is a puppet. That's not correct. If I don't want to cooperate and permit the Holy Spirit to speak through me, he won't be able to say anything, at least not through me. Let me say that again: I have the power to keep God quiet. We all do. That's how prophesying works.

The scriptures bear this out. This is true in the other realms of our walk with God, not just in the gift of prophesying. For example, if I don't want to pause and give thanks to God, he won't make me. If I refuse to acknowledge my sins, he won't make me. If I won't take time to pray, he won't make me. If I refuse to profess Jesus Christ is my Lord, he won't make me. He could, but he won't. He loves us too much. All of these things require us to open our mouths and speak. We are not puppets. We are persons with a free will. God wants us to do these things because we love him and we desire to relate to him.

Regarding prophecy, the scriptures say that the spirits of the prophets *are subject to* the prophets. In other words, God doesn't take over and force you to speak in tongues or prophesy. It is always under your control. We can manage our spirit.

For you can all prophesy one by one, so that all may learn and all may be exhorted; and the spirits of prophets are subject to prophets; for God is not a God of confusion but of peace... 1 Cor 14:31-32. Prophecy helps us learn more of God's thoughts and God's ways. (see Isaiah 55:8-9) The gift of prophecy builds us up. Paul said we could take turns prophesying to one another.

Paul said prophecy was an act of his will. *What is the outcome then? I will pray with the spirit and I will pray with the mind also; I will sing with the spirit and I will sing with the mind also.* 1 Cor 14:15-16

Notice the contrast? Paul said he could choose to yield to the Spirit as he wished as an act of will. "*I will* pray with the spirit" This was his regenerated human spirit empowered by the Holy Spirit praying, versus him praying with his trained human intellect. He could do either or both. Personally, I sometimes enjoying singing in the Spirit. It's a restful, enjoyable way to worship the Lord. It edifies me. God seems to enjoy it.

Because speaking or talking is something we can choose to do or choose not to do, all of the verbal operations of the Spirit require divine-human cooperation. It is a partnership. Therefore, it is a fact that prophetic gifts may be muzzled or quenched. It is also true that such gifts may be fanned into flames or stirred up. They can come alive, be reactivated. The choice is ours.

I think a good way for any Christian to start this process is to begin with rejoicing in the Lord. Give thanks. Believe that it is God's will for you to be able to express the Spirit of God through your mouth. Begin with praising God aloud.

Rejoice always; pray without ceasing; in everything give thanks; for this is God's will for you in Christ Jesus. Do not quench the Spirit; do not despise prophetic utterances. But examine everything carefully; hold fast to that which is good. (1 Thess 5:16-21) This verse says that these four things are the will of God for us: rejoicing, praying, giving thanks, and prophesying.

DEGREES OF GRACE

IN MY EXPERIENCE, and I think the scriptures bear this out, there are at least three levels of prophetic grace. The first and simplest is this: 1) <u>all believers</u> may occasionally prophesy by the Spirit. *"You may all prophesy one by one."* I place this level in the area called *"the spirit of prophecy."* By that I mean, the manifest presence of God is strong enough and the anointing upon a group is powerful enough so everyone there in that moment can prophesy. The second is: 2) the <u>gift of prophecy</u>. This is when the ability to prophesy is frequently operating in the life of a believer. This is the charismatic gift that a Spirit-filled person possesses. Third: 3) <u>a person becomes a prophet</u>. This takes years. God trusts them with authoritative words or high-level revelation. Leaders seek their counsel. They have credibility in the church and among other prophets. They will be known by the local elders or apostles. They may teach or train others with their classes or books. They impart prophetic grace.

In the Old Testament, the Holy Spirit came upon Saul and he prophesied. People said, *"Is Saul also among the prophets?"* However, he never prophesied again. He didn't have the gift. He wasn't in that office. It was a one-time event. (1 Sam 10:11) It confirmed that the prophet Samuel was right. Saul was chosen to be king. He had a chance to rule but his character fell short.

The gift of prophecy is very often present right after a person receives the baptism in the Holy Spirit. It is an overflowing of the Spirit. Here is an instance in the New Testament scriptures.

It happened that while Apollos was at Corinth, Paul passed through the upper country and came to Ephesus and found some disciples. He said to them, "Did you receive the Holy Spirit when you believed?" And they said to him, "No, we have not even heard whether there is a Holy Spirit." And he said, "Into what then were you baptized?" And they said, "Into John's baptism." Paul said, "John baptized with the baptism of repentance, telling the people to believe in Him who was coming after him, that is, in Jesus." When they heard this, they were baptized in the name of the Lord Jesus. And when Paul had laid his hands upon them, the Holy Spirit came on them, and they began speaking with tongues and prophesying. There were in all about twelve men. Acts 19:1-7

In another place, Paul said Christians (those who are Spirit-filled) could prophesy. *For you can all prophesy one by one, so that all may learn and all may be exhorted...* 1 Cor 14:31. This is a manifestation of the Spirit. In private, it gives personal edification. In public, it is for the common good. In church it is meant to bless your fellow believers. This happens among us as the Spirit overflows out through each of us in prayer, praise, tongues and prophecy.

There are varying degrees of authority, insight, and clarity in prophetic words. Some words carry more weight. This is based on the kind of word that God is releasing and to a degree, the faith and ability of the person who is speaking it. The power of the anointing can even vary from instance to instance. Usually, prophets will have more revelation and thus carry more authority.

As each one has received a special gift, employ it in serving one another as good stewards of the manifold grace of God. Whoever speaks, is to do so as one who is speaking the utterances of God; whoever serves is to do so as one who is serving by the strength which God supplies; so that in all things God may be glorified through Jesus Christ, to whom belongs the glory and dominion forever and ever. Amen. 1 Pet 4:10-11

PROPHETIC PRAYING

I THINK WE DOWNPLAY the role of unknown tongues in our prayer life because we misunderstand its private versus public use. For me, the main use of tongues is for my personal edification. I frequently need to be built up, at least daily. This use is in the category of "all kinds of prayer" that's mentioned in Ephesians six.

And take the helmet of salvation, and the sword of the Spirit, which is the word of God. With all prayer and petition pray at all times in the Spirit... (Eph 6:17-18) The apostle Jude said that praying like this builds up your faith. *But you, beloved, building yourselves up on your most holy faith, praying in the Holy Spirit...* Jude 1:20

When we are filled with the Spirit, whether we feel spiritual or not, we can always prophesy by faith. Faith is not a feeling. *Since we have gifts that differ according to the grace given to us, each of us is to exercise them accordingly: if prophecy, according to the proportion of his faith...* Romans 12:6

Let me unpack this weighty verse. First notice that we have gifts that differ. My gifts don't need to be the same or yours. Next, notice that gifts come according to grace. And, they arrive in our lives by faith. They are not earned or deserved, nor are they our wages. All the gifts are according to something that only God can provide, grace. Grace was paid for by Jesus but is appropriated by our faith. Next, notice that gifts need to be exercised by faith.

You must do something so that your gift operates. If you don't, it will remain dormant, merely spiritual potential instead of realized power. *God can equip the man with the gift but we have to man the equipment.* It is an act of divine-human cooperation. What God gives by grace we receive by faith. What we receive must be stirred up and used by faith. By faith, we can prophesy. There's no other way. We've got to work it.

Furthermore, there are varying degrees of anointing by the Spirit. Be anointed before you try to prophesy. Don't speak apart from the Holy Spirit's presence and prompting. There are varying degrees of anointing for each of the gifts. Some believers will have greater power to function than others. God's will and their yielding comes into play. The scripture sometimes says that *"great grace was on them."* This means that at other times believers had lesser amounts of grace. Greater grace is often associated with great generosity. Finally, notice this insightful phrase, *"the proportion of his faith."*

THE ROLE OF FAITH

PROPHECY IS PROPORTIONAL. Believers may have a different level of faith at different times and in different circumstances. This proportional faith is a factor because we can only prophesy successfully according to our degree (amount) of faith. Faith is always present tense. But it changes from day to day. I have a portion of faith that often allows me to prophesy spontaneously to a large congregation. In my life, this is related to hearing a word or seeing a word. What follows naturally is saying a word.

You may have a portion of faith that allows you to discretely write out a note and hand it secretly to an usher to give to the pastor for his later consideration. By the way, I've done that. I recently met a pastor I hadn't seen in years. He greeted me and said, *"You changed my life!"* He told me the note I'd sent to him while sitting on the back row in his church one Sunday morning ten years ago was still laying on his desk where he could see it. He said it was a word that profoundly altered his ministry.

My reaction? I praised God! It amazes me how awesome God is. I can't figure this stuff out. It's beyond my ability. It's proof that we're tapping into a timeless source of divine information from a Living God. By the grace of Christ and our fellowship of the Spirit, we can spiritually tune in by a hearing ear to a frequency of the Lord, like phoning home, and discover *"plans formed long ago in perfect faithfulness"* (Isaiah 25:1), plans that the Lord has tailored just for us.

As I said, there are degrees of grace. This is something you can only realize with experience. It certainly seems real. It fits what I see happening. Some people prophesy words of knowledge with startling details. Others confirm callings and ministries. Some only speak words that powerfully exhort and encourage. Others seem able to address matters of the heart, healing invisible wounds, curing abuse or rejection, affirming the Father's love. Some can address issues of church government or order, which I've done frequently. All of this variety is valid.

The point is the same person, on different days, in different places, can have different levels of faith, grace, anointing, or revelatory capacity. This is not a machine at work. It is not magic. It is the mystery of the Spirit of God using imperfect people to show forth God's flawless grace in different measures.

Let me summarize a few points. All spiritual gifts, including prophecy, are by grace. They do not come by merit. They are undeserved and are not proof of maturity or even accuracy. *For by grace you have been saved through faith; and that not of yourselves, it is the gift of God; not as a result of works, so that no one may boast.* (Eph 2:8-9) There is a principle here about how grace and faith are related. The faith which enabled you to first receive and then later operate spiritual gifts, is itself a gift of grace. Faith comes by hearing. Faith can grow and increase. God set the stage for you to be able to have faith. He opened your ears to hear his word. He gave you grace to repent and believe. The "first cause" is always God's grace. His grace precedes us throughout life to help us.

Don't be puffed up just because you are able to minister spiritual gifts. Keep a sober assessment of yourself. Be able to laugh at your mistakes. Realize that everything you have was given to you by the Lord. The measure of faith that you may move in was determined for you by the Lord. He sets the boundaries. He entrusts you with faith and gifts for his purpose. He knows you're not perfect. He chose you in advance knowing all the dumb things you would do. His anointing and our faith pair up to produce miracles. Faith is a loan given to us from our heavenly Father so we can succeed in his family business. *For through the grace given to me I say to everyone among you not to think more highly of himself than he ought to think; but to think so as to have sound judgment, as God has allotted to each a measure of faith.* Rom 12:3

A THEOLOGY OF GIFTS

GOD IS A GIVER. He is a rewarder. He responds to those who seek him. *And without faith it is impossible to please Him, for he who comes to God must believe that He is and that He is a rewarder of those who seek Him.* (Hebrews 11:6) When God sees our sincere heart, our hunger, our humility, our faith in him, he rewards us with gifts. God has tremendous affection for each of us and loves to bless us. The first gift he blesses us with is his presence.

Every member of the Trinity (the Adorable Godhead: Father, Son, and Holy Spirit) are gift-givers. The Father gave the Son to the world to save us and to redeem us. *For God so loved the world, that He gave His only begotten Son, that whoever believes in Him shall not perish, but have eternal life.* (John 3:16) When God gives a gift, he gives the best that heaven has to offer.

Jesus is a liberal giver. When he comes into our life, he gives us freedom from bondage to Satan and deliverance from dark spirits. He illuminates our minds. The light of God, the truth of the scriptures, the reality of his glorious kingdom comes in. Jesus lifts us out of shame and condemnation, gives us sonship, and shares with us his joy in knowing the Father. Besides saving us, he doesn't stop there: he gives us his Spirit. He pours out the Holy Spirit on us. I say, *"All this and heaven too!"*

The Holy Spirit is a great gift. *Repent and be baptized every one of you in the name of Jesus Christ for the forgiveness of your sins, and you will* **receive the gift** *of the Holy Spirit.* Acts 2:39 ESV

He is the promise of the Father. When the Holy Spirit comes, he brings not only his presence, companionship, and affirmation, but he provides us with constant coaching, reminders. We're not alone, ever. Then he gives us lesser gifts, his gracelets, that animate our mission for Jesus. These charismatic gifts help us reproduce in some small measure Christ's full venue of spiritual power and mercy toward people. The gifts that the Spirit brings include specific classes or manifestations: verbal gifts, power gifts, and revelatory gifts. Among these are healings, miracles, supernatural faith, tongues, interpretations, prophecies, words of knowledge, words of wisdom, and discerning of spirits. Besides that, the Spirit anoints our talent, training, knowledge, ability, and skills so that we can glorify God in every way possible.

DESIRING TO PROPHESY

ONE OF THE BIG theological questions I've wrestled with in my life and ministry is this: *How much is God's part and how much is my part?* We all want to do God's will, correct? But can God's will be done apart from my choices and actions? How much of what happens next depends on me? Isn't God in control? The answer is, "yes, but..." This question touches on how we approach our role in God's world. If God manages everything, then I don't need to do anything. I can just say "The will of God be done" and walk away. I don't need to pray. I don't need to fast. I don't need to give. I don't need to witness. If God wants them saved, he'll save them. If God wants them healed, he'll heal them. After all, God is in control, right? Wrong. That's not how his kingdom works.

In the kingdom of God, we are heirs together with Christ Jesus. We are also laborers together with the Lord. *For we are God's fellow workers; you are God's field, God's building.* (1 Cor 3:9) We team up with God to get the work of his kingdom done.[8] We can even pray for his kingdom to come on the earth. (Mt 6:33)

We have our part to play and it's an important part. That's why we're told that God's plan for us is to desire spiritual gifts, especially prophecy. We are encouraged to earnestly seek this particular gift. *Pursue love, yet desire earnestly spiritual gifts, but especially that you may prophesy. (1 Cor 14:1) Therefore, my brethren, **desire earnestly to prophesy...** (v 39).*

I think many Christians are afraid to desire something. They think of desire in the category of lust, like desire is love gone bad. They've been taught to fear wanting anything strongly. Yes, coveting something that is *not* yours is a sin. *"Thou shalt not covet."* But if I want to be with my wife, that's my right. God has given her to me. There is no sin in that. But if I want to take another man's wife, that's wrong! It isn't the desire itself that's wrong, it's only misplaced desire that's wrong. Coveting, craving, wanting something strongly that is mine or was promised to me is never wrong. That is merely exercising my privilege as a son or a daughter of the Great King. I think we Christians need to *covet* more! We need to redirect our passion toward the things of Christ. Seek first what is above. Go after what God promised. We need to be jealous for God's glory and earnestly pursue his gifts.

---

[8] I've written about the importance of ministry teams in *Emerging Apostles in the Developing Church* available on Amazon.com.

This understanding about expressing our desires to God is a key idea. This concept places the absence of spiritual gifts squarely in our lap. We have a responsibility here. The apostle James said, *"You have not because you ask not."* (James 4:2) Jesus said ask, seek, knock. Be persistent. *Ask, and it will be given to you; seek, and you will find; knock, and it will be opened to you.* Matt 7:7

Jesus explained to his disciples that they had a key role to play in acquiring things in God's kingdom. *And Jesus *answered saying to them, "Have faith in God. Truly I say to you, whoever says to this mountain, 'Be taken up and cast into the sea,' and does not doubt in his heart, but believes that what he says is going to happen, it will be granted him. Therefore I say to you, **all things for which you pray and ask,** believe that you have received them, and they will be granted you.* (Mark 11:22-24) What things are you praying and asking for? Look at your list of things you desire. How badly do you want it?

*And Jesus stopped and called them, and said, "What do you want Me to do for you?" They *said to Him, "Lord, we want our eyes to be opened." Moved with compassion, Jesus touched their eyes; and immediately they regained their sight and followed Him.* (Matt 20:32) This story is incredible! Jesus asking a blind man what he wanted done for him. I take this to mean that God really, really wants you to express your desires to him. Let me ask you: Do you know what you want? Get specific. Ask Jesus for it. Don't be passive. Pursue it with all your heart.

As you seek after the gift of hearing the Spirit or desire the ability to speak words by the Spirit, take comfort in knowing that the gift is always freely given. This gift comes to young and old, men and women.

> *'And it shall be in the last days,' God says,*
> *'That I will pour forth of MY Spirit on all mankind;*
> *And your sons and your daughters shall prophesy,*
> *And your young men shall see visions,*
> *And your old men shall dream dreams;*
> *Even on MY bondslaves, both men and women,*
> *I will in those days pour forth of MY Spirit*
> *And they shall prophesy.* Acts 2:17-18

I believe the gift of prophesying is more common than we think. It is perhaps an unconscious grace that needs to be sanctified, ignited by the anointing, and become biblically informed. How many young people might be musing alone? Perhaps they're hiding in their bedroom trying to cope with life's confusion. They start to imagine what life might be like one day. Perhaps a song starts to waft across their emotions, a stirring or a melody with a voice they can almost hear. Suddenly thoughts unbidden come into their mind. They see a picture that stirs hope or feeds ambition, a promise yet unfulfilled, a noble dream long forgotten. They hear words that sound like their own thoughts, so very familiar, but speaking of wildly optimistic plans.

It could very well be that their Father in heaven is prompting them to think of what he has dreamed for them, a prophecy of their possible inheritance among the redeemed. The God of the possible is removing the scales of blindness, speaking into existence what might yet be. God is brooding over this generation. Is it possible? If God speaks it, all things are possible. I believe more people than we ever imagined are meant to be prophetic. The youth are his. Mankind feels his Spirit.

Sadly, many of the next generation of young prophets have already been aborted in their mother's wombs. Their voices for God are silenced. They will never sing the songs of the Spirit.

EMERGING PROPHETS

ONE OF THE IMPORTANT roles of the Holy Spirit is that he works with Jesus to point out new ministers God is calling. How does he do this? He uses his "prophetic pointer," a prophet or a prophecy designating someone by means of a spoken word. This assists senior leaders so they can give intense training to new emerging leaders.

Something like this happened in the church in Antioch as they waited expectantly in prayer until the Spirit spoke to them. It's important to note that Antioch wasn't founded by an apostle. This key time of prayer included prophets and teachers who were working in Antioch. No apostles were present. God threw the door of gospel expansion wide open for the Gentiles after this event in Acts 13. For the first time, the reproductive cycle of the church was fully engaged. The elders (these prophets and teachers) of the church in Antioch sent out an apostolic team. It all depended on the Holy Spirit speaking.

*Now there were at Antioch, in the church that was there, **prophets and teachers**: Barnabas, and Simeon who was called Niger, and Lucius of Cyrene, and Manaen who had been brought up with Herod the tetrarch, and Saul. While they were ministering to the Lord and fasting, **the Holy Spirit said,** "Set apart for Me Barnabas and Saul for the work to which I have called them." Then, when they had fasted and prayed and laid their hands on them, they sent them away. So, **being sent out by the Holy Spirit**....* (Acts 13:1-4)

This is a very important reason that prophets are needed in the church today. We have not yet finished the Great Commission. We need his help in raising up more laborers. We have a job to do. *And Jesus came up and spoke to them, saying, "All authority has been given to Me in heaven and on earth. Go therefore and make disciples of all the nations, baptizing them in the name of the Father and the Son and the Holy Spirit, teaching them to observe all that I commanded you; and lo, I am with you always, even to the end of the age."* Matt 28:18-20

I've already said that in the New Testament era, prophets lay foundations. (Eph 2:20) I think this is especially true when they work with apostles and teachers. Prophets help get the church grounded and off to a good start. They help make sure that the ongoing supernatural work of the Holy Spirit – sigs, wonders, and miracles - are part of the church's foundation.

The old notion of someone in a ragged toga who wears sandals and holds up a sign saying, "the end of the world is near!" is an outdated image. Now, they may not be in a suit, that's for sure. But they're not a renegade or an outcast that lives in a cave. One of my favorite prophets was a quiet man who loved the Bible, led the choir at church, and worked for decades at Ethyl Corporation as a bookkeeper. His name was Leon Price. He is in heaven today. I dearly miss him. If you met Leon for the first time, you would have liked him and trusted him. And yes, he would have been wearing a suit. He liked to dress up. He wore a suit almost every day.

Leon had a word for apostles and pastors. It was this: *"Make love the main thing!"* He always had a word for people he met during the course of the day. He told me, *"I've never met anyone but what the Lord had something to say to them."* His words always edified, encouraged, called people up, and pointed them to faith in Jesus. He once prophesied to a drunk who sat in the back of my church, "You're a man of God!" He once prophesied on Sunday to a runaway teen I'd located and returned to his parents on Saturday... "Son, you can't run away from God!"

The gift of prophecy or the ministry of prophets can be exciting. People listening to them can be amazed. Because of this, pastors need to be wise shepherds when this occurs, to guide the flock in paths of rejoicing along with peace. Don't chase the spectacular. Focus on faith hope and love. Pursue righteousness. Stay in the word. Work at fitting this wonderful ministry into the context of the church's whole expression of Jesus, especially our corporate body life.

Prophets don't purposely misbehave. They don't try to disrupt the church. God loves for things to be decent and in order. Generally, prophets honor apostles. They respect bishops and elders. The work with pastors. They sit in a council with apostles or elders when they are invited. Here is an example of this. *Therefore, I exhort the elders among you, as your fellow elder* (i.e.- sum-presbuteros) *and witness of the sufferings of Christ, and a partaker also of the glory that is to be revealed, shepherd the flock of God among you, exercising oversight not under compulsion, but voluntarily...* (1 Pet 5:1-2)

Prophets are the best encouragers in the world! *Judas and Silas, also being prophets themselves, encouraged and strengthened the brethren with a lengthy message.* (Acts 15:32) Prophets of God build people up. They don't tear down. They establish present truth for the church and represent Jesus among the saints. I think prophets are a comfort to the church. Of course, sometimes their peculiar role is to afflict the comfortable and comfort the afflicted.

I think by now you can see that the office of the prophet is meant to help establish the church and bear witness to truth. Prophets are part of an essential foundation in the body of Christ on the earth. They carry great grace, a rich deposit of the knowledge of the Lord. They are special because of who they represent – Jesus – not their talent or training. Some prophets are amazing, being highly respected in heaven, but they're not very good teachers or preachers on earth. That's okay. We need all kinds. Prophets are who they are by the grace of God.

But by the grace of God I am what I am, and His grace toward me did not prove vain; but I labored even more than all of them, yet not I, but the grace of God with me. (1 Cor 15:10) When we honor prophets, we honor the Lord who sent them. We honor God's grace on them.

We should receive prophets because they can bless us. *He who receives a prophet in the name of a prophet shall receive **a prophet's reward...*** (Matt 10:41)

The principle here is that prophets must be received in order for their gift to function properly. Is the prophet respected and received as a prophet in the house? There are some churches where I'm given room to be myself. In other churches, if I should visit, I'm not able to wear my mantle, so I behave myself. I do my best to keep quiet. Why? I know they won't receive any word I share (for a variety of possible reasons). I've learned that if I'm not given an unction to speak by the Spirit, or if I'm not invited, or won't be received, I don't even try.

I once went a whole week at a special conference, overseas, teaching the word, but not given any liberty from God to utter prophetic words. This was so unusual for me. And I was billed as the prophet at the conference! Well, I did have one loud proclamation at the start of the conference. *"Someone here is stealing money. If you put it back, the Lord says he won't uncover you."* No one claimed that word for themself. By the end of the week, I wondered what was wrong with me. Was I spiritually deaf? Had I grieved the Lord? But the Lord showed me that it wasn't me. In fact, the last day of the conference the Lord gave me the name of my waiter as he approached my table. The Lord even pronounced it and then spelled it out for me- *"Ibrahim."* I hadn't gone spiritually deaf!

Prophets can be odd ducks. We need to be patient with them. Many prophets have been rebuffed or rejected, misunderstood and mistreated. Once you cultivate a relationship with a prophet, keep them close to your heart. Pray for them. Love them, Value them. Make sure their needs are met. Be their friend. Give them a spiritual home. Don't mistreat them like the stubborn Israelites once did. You don't need to flatter them, just listen to them when they get your attention. You'll be glad you did.

Blessed are you when men hate you, and ostracize you, and insult you, and scorn your name as evil, for the sake of the Son of Man. Be glad in that day and leap for joy, for behold, your reward is great in heaven. **For in the same way their fathers used to treat the prophets.** *But woe to you who are rich, for you are receiving your comfort in full. Woe to you who are well-fed now, for you shall be hungry. Woe to you who laugh now, for you shall mourn and weep. Woe to you when all men speak well of you, for* **their fathers used to treat the false prophets in the same way.** Luke 6:22-26

PROPHETS ENDURE STUFF

MANY PROPHETS NEED to be healed of verbal wounds from rejection. They carry hidden scars. They've had it tough in the ministry whereas pastors are often cared for. Pastors have a recognized position. Prophets don't seem to fit anywhere. Perhaps that's why some prophets come across angry, which they shouldn't be doing. Maybe they've been stoned by "sweet" Christians. I say, never preach at a church with a pile of rocks outside the door!

There are false prophets. We must discern between true and false prophets. In the Old Testament, God's people were warned to judge the prophet. If a prophet's word failed to come true, he was not to be feared. He perhaps was even to be stoned. In the New Testament, the office functions differently. We are to judge the prophecy (the word spoken, the utterance), not judge the person speaking it. All persons prophesying will miss the mark at some time. That doesn't make them false or counterfeit.

If you are a leader and a powerful word is released to you, immediately evaluate it. Even if they said, "Thus saith the Lord!" you still need to judge their word. Were they sent by God? To you? Was the word on target?

"I did not send these prophets, but they ran. I did not speak to them, but they prophesied. "But if they had stood in My council, then they would have announced My words to My people and would have turned them back from their evil way and from the evil of their deeds. Jeremiah 23:21-22

There is nothing more powerful on the face of the earth than someone who has heard a word directly from the throne of God and been sent to speak it to people on the earth. God appoints us to a people, to a place, and to a purpose. Prophets help us identify those things. Prophets stand in the counsel of the Lord. That is their source of authority for being sent with a word.

> *The Spirit of the Lord will rest on Him,*
> *The spirit of wisdom and understanding,*
> *The spirit of counsel and strength,*
> *The spirit of knowledge and the fear of the Lord.*
> Isaiah 11:2

Real prophets are known and approved by their fruit. I mentioned earlier my friend Leon Price. I can testify that he displayed Christ-like character all the time. You could see the fruit of the Spirit in Leon's life, including kindness and faithfulness. He walked with Jesus. This ought to be true for everyone who carries this grace. Gifts are validated by our fruit. Be a fruit inspector.

*"Beware of the false prophets, who come to you in sheep's clothing, but **inwardly are ravenous wolves.** You will **know them by their fruits**. Grapes are not gathered from thorn bushes nor figs from thistles, are they? So every good tree bears good fruit, but the bad tree bears bad fruit. A good tree cannot produce bad fruit, nor can a bad tree produce good fruit. Every tree that does not bear good fruit is cut down and thrown into the fire. So then, you will know them by their fruits.* Matthew 7:15-20

Mature prophets are willing to be examined. Ask them, *"Are you willing for your words to be evaluated?"* Public prophesies should be evaluated publicly. Bad words that didn't come true should not be allowed to be forgotten or swept under the rug. Make it a teachable moment. Where is the accountability? I know a fine pastor whose church got burned by a prophet who predicted Hillary Clinton would win the 2016 election. The prophet said it on a Sunday morning as a guest speaker. The whole church is now skeptical about prophets. The prophet never confessed his error or admitted his mistake. This doesn't mean that he was a false prophet, but it does mean that this particular prophecy was not true. Let's be honest brokers of this grace. The church deserves better.

Wrong words can happen if someone gets careless, or carnal, or channels a wrong spirit. The prophet needs to repent, especially if they had unholy or evil motives. Perhaps they prophesied out of their own imagination.

Then the word of the Lord came to me saying, "Son of man, prophesy against the prophets of Israel who prophesy, and say to those who prophesy from their own inspiration, 'Listen to the word of the Lord! Thus says the Lord God, **"Woe to the foolish prophets who are following their own spirit and have seen nothing.** Ezekiel 13:1-3

While genuine prophets operate by the grace of God and under the inspiration of the Holy Spirit, false prophets manifest a counterfeit anointing. Their motives are wicked. This is the work of an unholy spirit. False prophecies have various sources. They can be soulish, or psychic, or even Satanic. *This wisdom is not that which comes down from above, but is earthly, natural, demonic. For where jealousy and selfish ambition exist, there is disorder and every evil thing. But the wisdom from above is first pure, then peaceable, gentle, reasonable, full of mercy and good fruits, unwavering, without hypocrisy.* (James 3:15-17) All channeling, seances, witchcraft, or fortune-telling (if it is real and not merely a show) is done by false prophets by means of a lying spirit pretending to be God. They purvey false wisdom. Their intent is to manipulate and deceive. They are not to be feared.

EVALUATING PROPHECIES

HOW DO WE JUDGE genuine prophetic words in the church? Evaluating Spirit-words is essential. We need a protocol, a framework, which I will now share with you. If we don't judge prophecies, we *will* despise them, and we are urged not to despise prophecies. *...do not despise prophetic utterances.* (1 Thess 5:20) To despise something is to disrespect, devalue, disdain, dismiss, put down, or make light of. In the modern church era, we tend to despise a prophecy if it did not come from the platform. It was not delivered by an ordained "full time" preacher since it didn't come from the pastor. If you ignore a good prophetic word you may have skipped right past an open door to a divine blessing.

By the way, I think we need to get rid of the words *full time ministry* because of its innate bias. This phrase exhibits prejudice. It neglects the role of body ministry from the members. It elevates the artificial title of clergy over laity, which God hates. (Rev 2:6) The fact is, the body of believers, not the clergy, is where the majority of spiritual gifts reside. Let God's saints freely speak!

Here is a simple protocol or a pattern for evaluating prophetic words. Right up front you should know that you are free to at any time, when receiving a prophetic word, to conclude that the word you heard was not right for you. You can say without condemnation, "I don't agree with that word." Or perhaps, "I don't see it." My advice in that case is to put it on a shelf for now and pray about it.

Prophetic words should be received in the context of relationships. We are set by Christ into a certain place in his body for a reason. You find your function by where you fit. You should be surrounded by trusted Christians, brothers and sisters whom you know, respect and love. *But now God has placed the members, each one of them, **in the body,** just as He desired.* (1 Cor 12:18) Do I know the person who spoke prophesied to me? If I don't know them personally or know the quality of their walk with Christ and trust their gift, do my elders know them?

You may ignore strangers. *But we request of you, brethren, that you appreciate those who diligently **labor among you,** and have charge over you in the Lord and give you instruction, and that you **esteem them very highly in love because of their work.*** (1 Thess 5:12-13)

Spiritual gifts should operate primarily within the context of the body of believers, where the words can be heard by everyone and evaluated. Who is it among you that spoke? If they weren't from among you, what is their reputation? *A **stranger** they simply will not follow, but will flee from him, because they do not know the voice of strangers.* (John 10:5) This doesn't mean that a gifted person who is new in your meeting, or a prophet who is visiting among you, may not prophesy to you. It simply means you are free to evaluate the word based on your acknowledging their reputation and credibility.

When you listen to a prophetic word, does your spirit bear witness to it? Is there peace in your heart with what is being said? You can rely on the Holy Spirit to reassure your heart. He is inside you in your spirit and he will either tell you he is excited or tell you he is not happy. Pay attention to this. You are discerning something. *The Spirit Himself **testifies with our spirit** that we are children of God.* Rom 8:16

Beyond subjective feelings or internal discernment by your spirit, what are the facts that are being revealed or told? Is there something being said that is true to your history or is it false? Here is where you can inquire of those around you. Do mature saints agree with what you heard? *Let two or three prophets speak, and **let the others pass judgment.*** 1 Cor 14:29

Of course, the premier standard for evaluating all prophetic utterances are the historical scriptures. What does the Bible say? The written will supersede any spoken word. *Now these were more noble-minded than those in Thessalonica, for they received the word with great eagerness, **examining the Scriptures daily** to see whether these things were so.* Acts 17:11

*But know this first of all, that no **prophecy of Scripture** is a matter of one's own interpretation, for no prophecy was ever made by an act of human will, but men moved by the Holy Spirit spoke from God.* (2 Pet 1:20) The words of our Holy Bible are prophecies. They were inspired by the Spirit. They have been refined seven times in the fire like silver or gold with the dross removed. They are superior to our fallible efforts to prophesy.

The scriptures are the real thing. God figured it out even if we can't understand it all. Knowing this about the scriptures, it is still possible for people to misinterpret the written word and therefore mis-apply the word to situations. Don't go off the deep end, either from a written word, or from a prophetic word.[9]

Once you have passed this far in evaluating a prophetic word, and you can conclude that the Spirit of God is indicating something to you. What do you do next? Take your time. For example, don't quit your job and sell

---

[9] For a lesson on how to interpret scriptures in the Bible, see my book *Knowing God's Word*. It has an excellent section on exegesis.

your house because someone told you that you're called to go to Russia. First of all, are you called to go to Russia? You'll know it if you are. Second, there is always a process involved. Don't be hasty. This may take years. You need endorsement (being sent), planning, provision, and then you need to be received on the Russia end of things. Don't interpret any word privately. That's the reason why parking lot prophecies are not wise. Where are the witnesses to help you evaluate what was said?

The exception to this is when a word of knowledge is being used by God as part of witnessing. This is in the context of evangelism. This kind of word is exciting. It often leads to dramatic conversions. It can be done with total strangers as the Lord leads. A wise way to do it is to say to them, "Do you mind if I ask you a question? I'm a Christian. Sometimes the Lord shows me things. Do you....?" Go on from there to share your word of knowledge with them. Always ask if you can pray with them to receive Jesus as their Savior. Trust God that he had them ready for this divine encounter. Take a chance!

Back to evaluating your word... as far as walking out any word you've received from the Lord, use sanctified common sense. The Lord will never violate your conscience or your convictions. God won't ask you to do something contrary to the values he himself has taught you. He won't ask you to do something you believe is immoral or unethical. This goes without saying but I said it anyway. He may lead you in a way that's unfamiliar or he may open up something to you that you didn't previously know was in the Bible, but that's different and it's okay.

My advice to anyone after they hear a word that gives guidance or direction, is to write it out, pray over it, and get counsel about it. If a vision, word, or prophecy affects the direction of your life, the welfare of your family, or the future direction of the church, by all means, submit it to leaders or <u>wait for confirmation</u>. Don't speak act or hastily. If it is a word for the church, always wait for the pastors or elders to sort things out. Don't go around spreading a word or vision that they haven't yet had time to process. Let them have the prerogative of fulfilling their leadership responsibility to God. Honor their role.

Don't interpret a word solo if it affects your family. If the word affects your ministry, <u>ask your spouse</u>. Take it to your pastor. Go to the elders for <u>counsel</u>. There is safety in two or three agreeing. Wisdom rests in those around you, so seek after it.

Always be quick to search the Bible for wisdom. The Holy Spirit will *never* <u>contradict the Scriptures</u>. They go hand in hand. The Word will back up the word. Genuine prophetic words fit into the flow of biblical history. They are compatible with God's nature. They harmonize with the whole counsel of scriptures.

Another general precaution. There is usually a *chronos* factor, the waiting that's involved when it comes to prophetic words being fulfilled. This means a *rhema* word takes time to be fulfilled. That's normal. The proper season needs to arrive for the word to become operative. Hey, Jesus was a nine-month baby! Don't try to make your word happen. Don't force it. Just pray. Wait on God. I'm still waiting on some words to be fulfilled that I received twenty years ago.

There are some things all of us can do to be better prepared for the arrival of the fullness of time. We can recall our prophetic words in prayer to God. I do this and then say, "God you didn't lie! I know your word is true!" Then I praise him in advance for doing what he promised. We can rehearse prophetic words to ourselves so as to build up our personal faith. We can practice the godly disciplines that we know we'll need in the future. Especially, we can grow in intimacy and fellowship with the Lord by waiting on him. By doing these things we can incubate our prophetic word until the vision is born.[10]

With experience, you'll learn how to handle prophetic words. They are always spoken in context. They need to be judged the same way. What is the Spirit is saying to the church? To me? God doesn't speak in a vacuum. You'll see how a prophetic person may have seen a true word, a real revelation, but how as a human being

---

[10] For more on this subject, read *Hearing God's Voice,* available at Amazon.com.

they might miss it a mile on the interpretation side. The error it is not God's fault. The person might be a PIT-*prophet in training.* At any rate, we are all learning how to prophesy, how to better express out loud what the Spirit is speaking in our hearts. Knowing this, we can handle prophetic utterances like a teachable moment. We can make room in the church for the gift of prophecy.

OTHER BOOKS AVAILABLE

Heaven's Angel Army

What part do angels play in answering our prayers? Do angels speak to us, guide us, give us dreams? What task do God's angels have in the end-time harvest? Can prophesying the word of God release holy angels to act on our behalf?

More Than Equals

What role do women have in the gospel ministry? Why did Paul have so many women on his apostolic team? Can women be leaders in the church? This intriguing exploration into the Scriptures dismantles the incorrect doctrines and misinterpretations that restrict women from serving Christ.

Deliverance - Our Legacy

Jesus' divine power sets captives free! Discover how using the power of the Holy Spirit and the authority of Jesus' name liberates people from needless demonic suffering. A biblically balanced teaching into this neglected topic. This book addresses necessary issues regarding the world, the flesh and the devil and explains how believers may minister deliverance.

Thief in the Storehouse

There is an evil plot to undermine our kingdom economy. The devil wants to keep Christians poor, keep churches broke, and prevent Christ's servants from fulfilling their high calling. Discover eye-opening truth as you tap into God's law of endless supply. With these God-ideas, you can evict the thief from your storehouse, gain control over your money, provide for your family, and honor God with your increasing wealth.

About the Author

Ron and Lana Wood were married in 1969 while at Southeastern University in Lakeland, Florida, where they studied Missions and Bible. They have two children and six grandchildren. They have served Assembly of God, Baptist, and non-denominational churches in the southeastern United States and were missionaries in Johannesburg, SA.

Ron founded Touched by Grace, an Arkansas non-profit corporation, in 1998. His books are published as a gospel resource for the maturing church to help teach, train, and equip believers for ministry within the body of Christ and to the world.

Follow Ron's Bible teaching or receive training through his YouTube videos, read his posts @touchedbygracenwa on Facebook, or find his articles at www.touchedbygrace.org. Donations to the work may be made through PayPal. Order Ron's books (Print or Kindle versions) at Amazon.com.

Made in the USA
Columbia, SC
31 May 2021